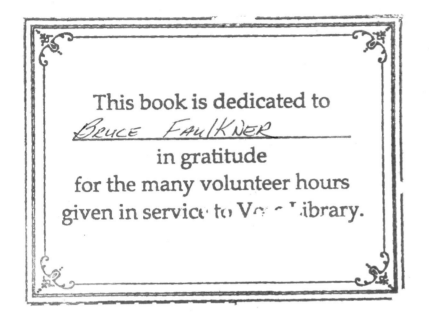

This book is dedicated to

Bruce Faulkner

in gratitude
for the many volunteer hours
given in service to Vose Library.

Confluence
Merrymeeting Bay

D1597073

Looking from the Abby mouth toward North Bath at high tide, late Occtober

Confluence
Merrymeeting Bay

Franklin Burroughs

Photography by

Heather Perry

Tilbury House Publishers

Gardiner, Maine

Tilbury House, Publishers
2 Mechanic Street
Gardiner, Maine 04345
800–582–1899 • www.tilburyhouse.com

First edition: August 2006 • 10 9 8 7 6 5 4 3 2 1

Library of Congress Cataloging-in-Publication Data
Burroughs, Franklin.
   Confluence : Merrymeeting Bay / Franklin Burroughs ; photography by
Heather Perry.-- 1st ed.
       p. cm.
   Includes bibliographical references and index.
   ISBN-13: 978-0-88448-282-6 (pb : alk. paper)
   ISBN-10: 0-88448-282-0 (pb : alk. paper)
   1. Natural history--Maine--Merrymeeting Bay. 2. Burroughs, Franklin.
I. Title.
   QH105.M2.B87 2006
   508.741'8--dc22
                          2006005681

Designed on Crummett Mountain by Edith Allard, Somerville, Maine
Copyediting by Barbara Diamond, A Word to the Wise, Litchfield, Maine
Color scans by Photocraft, Boulder, Colorado, and by Pure Photographic
Goodness, Portland, Maine
Printed and bound by Worzalla Publishing, Steven's Point, Wisconsin

For Linwood Rideout and Finn Perry Weafer

Wild rice, September

Contents

Preface   viii

Orientation   I

Revenant   9

Transcience and Evidence   I5

An Intimation of Immortality   2I

The Oldest Profession   29

The Microfishery   39

Remnants and Renewals   47

Newcomers   59

Tidings of Several Springs   65

Voices of the Turtle   85

Sowango   99

The Wild Crop   II9

Quabacook   I25

Hunter Education   I27

OGL and the OED   I49

Intelligent Design   I6I

The Wild Common   I79

I0/II   I9I

Confluence   I97

Preface

M**Y WIFE AND I CAME TO MAINE** in 1968, and I first
went out onto the Bay that fall. Since 1973, we have lived in
Bowdoinham, on the tidal portion of the Cathance—most
of that time in an old farmhouse about a mile from where
the river empties into the Bay; for the last three years in a
new house about another mile further upstream.

Of the towns around the Bay, Bowdoinham has much
the longest waterfront and, I think, feels the deepest sense
of ownership and connection. We regard it as the ancient
Romans regarded the Mediterranean: it is *Mare Nostrum,* OUR
inland sea. Like some other of my fellow citizens, I piddle
around on the Bay a good deal, usually with the pretext of
hunting—less often, of fishing, or paddling, or going out to
the Sands, the Riviera of Bowdoinham, for some swimming
or an evening picnic in the summer.

I've gained a sense of the human and natural history of
the Bay slowly and randomly, by a process more akin to
osmosis than to anything resembling research or systematic
observation. I have written about it off and on for twenty
years. For five years—from 1997 to 2002—I wrote about it
regularly, in short essays that were published in the quarterly

newsletter of the Friends of Merrymeeting Bay, a local land trust and conservation advocacy group that includes members from all around the Bay, but that is firmly centered in east Bowdoinham. This book draws heavily on those essays.

It also draws on conversations with a variety of people, whose experience and knowledge of the Bay exceed mine by light years. Some of them are mentioned in the essays that follow: Linwood Rideout, Ronnie Burrell, Buster Prout, Jim Brawn, Adelbert Temple, John Edgecomb, Jimmy McPherson, all of whom have hunted, fished, and knocked around on the Bay from their boyhoods, five or six or seven or eight decades ago. Some have been scientists, particularly John Lichter, a biologist in Bowdoin College's Environmental Studies Program. Some have simply had a long, multigenera-

tional experience of living around the Bay, observing it, noticing and remembering. Dana Cary comes especially to mind. And some are *sui generis,* even by Bowdoinham standards: David Berry, in other words.

The book has been underwritten by a grant from the Environmental Studies Program at Bowdoin; for his help in procuring it, I am indebted to the unfailing generosity and resourcefulness of DeWitt John, the Director of Environmental Studies.

This book would not have happened without the initial encouragement and sustained, energetic attention of Jennifer Bunting at Tilbury House.

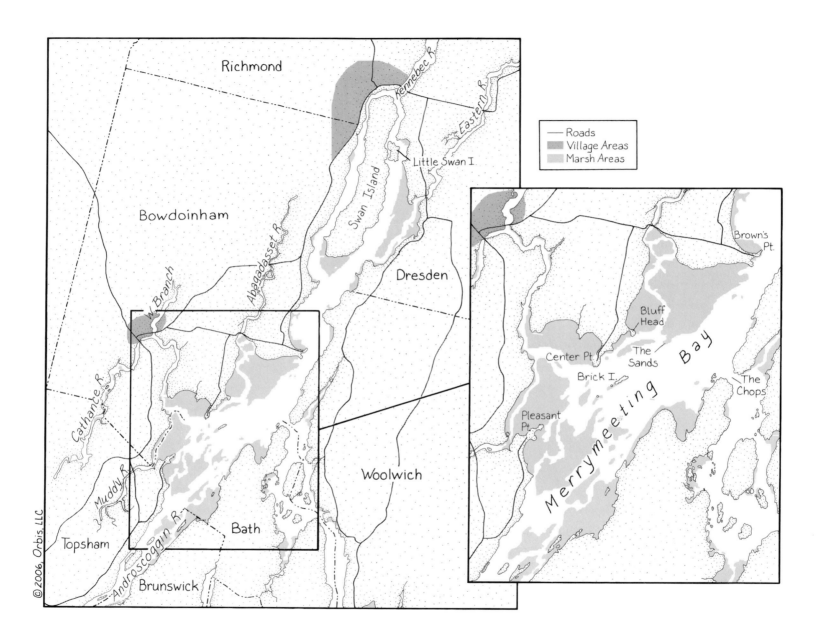

Roads
Village Areas
Marsh Areas

Richmond

Bowdoinham

Kennebec R.

Eastern R.

Swan Island

Little Swan I

Dresden

Abagadasset R.

W. Branch

Cathance R.

Muddy R.

Woolwich

Androscoggin R.

Topsham

Bath

Brunswick

Brown's Pt.

Bluff Head

Center Pt.

The Sands

Brick I.

Merrymeeting Bay

Pleasant Pt.

The Chops

Orientation

Rivers don't like to share the same delta. According to John McPhee, there are only four known places where two sizeable rivers, with entirely separate watersheds, converge at their mouths. The Sacramento and San Joaquin Rivers merge east of San Francisco Bay, where they have been diked and diverted, their marshes ditched, drained, and converted into some of this continent's most productive farmland. The Ganges and Brahmaputra Rivers combine their sacred waters in Bangladesh, essentially creating that low, flat, fertile, and flood-prone nation. The Tigris and Euphrates meet in south central Iraq, at the eastern edge of the Fertile Crescent. Their delta, a huge phragmites marsh, was for centuries home to the marsh Arabs, a highly distinctive and independent people until they and their habitat were improved out of existence by Saddam Hussein.

It is hardly surprising that these three places have loomed large in the economies and histories of their countries—indeed, two of them have loomed large in the history of what we call civilization. River deltas are typically places of great natural abundance, concentrations of nutrients, and therefore of fish, birds, and mammals, including ourselves. It stands to reason that a delta combining the wealth of two watersheds, nourishing marshes and swamps and deep alluvial soils, would be especially rich in natural history, and then in human history.

It is therefore surprising that the fourth of these unique places—about a mile from where I sit at this moment—Town of Bowdoinham, County of Sagadahoc, State of Maine—is known and celebrated and investigated by very few people indeed, and that, in sharp contrast to the other three, it has been only unintentionally modified by human agency. This place, of course, is Merrymeeting Bay, where the Kennebec, flowing directly south out of Moosehead Lake, and the Androscoggin, taking a more devious route south-eastward from Lake Umbagog, get their acts together. Even in Bowdoinham, I have encountered citizens whose conception of Merrymeeting Bay is hazy; and in Brunswick and Bath, both of which have considerable frontage on the Bay, the majority of the people I know who sail, kayak, swim, sunbathe, fish, walk, watch birds, and generally go in for *al fresco* recreations have heard persistent rumors about it, but have never gotten around to following them up. Or have perhaps seen it once, concluded that they had seen it all, and struck it off their lists.

As for the thousands of tourists who come to this region of Maine every summer, only a few hear anything about Merrymeeting Bay that would serve to distinguish it in their minds from Maquoit Bay, Middle Bay, Quahog Bay, and all the other involutions and indentations of the Maine coast. And those tourists who glance at maps to get a general impression of the lay of the land and see an irregularly shaped blotch of blue well inland from the sea could be for-given for assuming that it is a large lake, along the lines of Cobbosseecontee, Annabessacook, and Maranacook, a few miles to the northwest.

The tourists or unsuspecting natives who actually venture out onto the Bay find it peculiar. North, south, east, and west, it is to all appearances landlocked, surrounded by low ridges and wooded shores, with here and there a patch of pasture or tillage land, and a scattering of houses, most of them well back from the water and few of them new. In this regard it resembles a lake, and the water in it is unmistakably fresh—its marshes look nothing like the spartina marshes of the coast, and familiar freshwater plants—pickerel weed, arrowhead, cattails—grow in its shallows. With luck, a tourist there might see a muskrat or a beaver, further re-enforcing the lake effect.

But, with luck, the tourist might also see a seal. And he or she will certainly see that the place is tidal, full of cur-rents and countercurrents. Its water resembles neither the clear, cold waters of Casco Bay nor the almost equally clear, and somewhat less cold, waters of the splendid and much-touristed lakes of Maine's North Woods. It is turbid and warm, and might be perfectly acceptable in the less favored states south of here, but falls short of the Vacationland standard. The marshes, too, look exotic, like something you might see along the Nile. At low tide, they are higher than a man's head. The issue is not exactly whether they are beautiful or otherwise. The issue is that you never see anything remotely resembling them on the calendar covers and postcards, or in the brochures, magazines, and books that depict the natural glories of Maine. They do not suggest the tidy, stern, spare, and stark New England aesthetic that exists in the imagery of tourism and imagination of tourists, whether they come from elsewhere or are, so to speak, tourists-in-residence.

So these are two reasons for making a book about Merrymeeting Bay. In geomorphological and global terms, it is an extreme rarity. And it is, at the same time, a place that has been very largely overlooked—important to only a small percentage, within which Heather Perry and I include ourselves, of even the people who live with it in their backyards.

But the other reason for making the book is closer to the bone. People obviously have a natural and frequently disastrous instinct to seize, defend, and expand their literal or metaphorical turf, to claim a place for themselves. But we may also have a more elusive, because less competitive and aggressive, instinct, which is the longing to be claimed by a place—a neighborhood or a city, the vanished household of

Dresden: Eastern River

our childhood or scenes enriched by antiquities and historical associations. Tourism is built upon such longing, but can never offer it more than momentary satisfaction. Speaking for myself, this longing is generated by some places and not by others, and it involves some intimation that the place around me is something like an inhabitable narrative, one that stretches back into the natural and historical past, connecting it to the human and natural life of its present. It has the promise of any narrative—suspense, surprise, eventfulness, an atmosphere that sharpens attention and invites reflection. I hope the essays and photographs that follow will exemplify and clarify what I mean.

First, this much about the Bay itself. The map shows that its general orientation, like that of so many landforms in Maine—ridges, valleys, lakes, peninsulas, islands, sounds—is from north northeast to south southwest. It is bounded by Topsham, Bowdoinham, and Richmond on its west side, and by Brunswick, Bath, Woolwich, and Dresden on the east side. Swan Island, lying in the middle of the upper Bay, roughly four miles long and half a mile wide, was originally part of Dresden, but in 1847 it seceded and so became an eighth Merrymeeting municipality, taking for itself the resoundingly unevocative name of Perkins. Perkins sat in the Bay and lived out of it: ice-harvesting, shipbuilding, and fishing were its economy. Those trades supported a population that seems to have peaked at about a hundred souls. Perkins was also a port, of a sort: one ferry ran from its western shore to Richmond and another from its eastern shore to Dresden, so that all significant east-west traffic had to pass through the town, which undoubtedly brought it a little business and a lot of gossip, considerably mitigating its insularity. By the 1930s, pollution had killed the ice and fish harvesting, and wooden ships had died a natural death. In 1936 a bridge was built from Richmond to Dresden, half a mile north of the island, and the town died. Once abandoned, it was nominally annexed by Richmond, but the island itself, a beautiful and slightly haunting place, is now owned by the state's Department of Game and Inland Fisheries and populated chiefly by white-tailed deer. *Sic transit Perkins*, our local ghost town, an inhabited narrative no more.

But back to the Bay. The Androscoggin comes in from the south end; the Kennebec comes in from the north. On a falling tide, their waters run into each other. This is not an insignificant collision; the two rivers between them drain roughly a third of Maine, plus a bit of New Hampshire. Thus united, they pass out through the Chops, a narrow gap between two handsome headlands, one in north Bath and the other in Woolwich. The water is deep here—close to a hundred feet—but it does not look it. The constricted currents writhe, boil, and generate powerful eddies in midstream—they look like enormously magnified versions of the whirling vortexes created by a canoe paddle. When the tide is running out strongly, the whole river seems to slope downstream, as though you were approaching a mighty cataract. Once I saw a doe set out from the Bath side to swim across to Woolwich, 250 yards away. The tide was falling. She swam forward and she traveled sideways, like a turtle crossing a conveyor belt. She finally made landfall more than half a mile downstream, opposite Line's Island, scrambled out onto a ledgy shore, hoisted her tail, and capered off into the woods.

The Chops definitively, dramatically, and by universal consent marks the downstream boundary of Merrymeeting Bay. From here on down to the sea, sixteen miles as the sturgeon swims, one third of the running water in Maine, resuming the name of the Kennebec River, flows by the shipbuilding city of Bath, jogs east at Fiddler's Reach, passes between two guideposts for benighted souls—the beautiful old Phippsburg Church on the west bank and, directly opposite it, the Squirrel Point Lighthouse—and so on past Parker Head and the sand beach at Fort Popham, after which it goes under the name of the Atlantic Ocean. There are more handsome river corridors in the world, but having never seen them and being unable to imagine them, I suffer no feelings of deprivation.

It is harder to say exactly what and where the upstream limits of the Bay are. In addition to the Kennebec and the Androscoggin, four small rivers—the Muddy, Cathance, and Abagadasset (variously spelled and, because life is short, generally called the Abby) on the west side, and the Eastern on the east side—also feed into the Bay. At what point do they cease to be tidal rivers and become Merrymeeting Bay? The mouths of the four smaller rivers open rather abruptly into the Bay, and if you are paddling down one of them, the wooded shores on both sides, and the feeling of cozy enclosure they create, are quite dramatically replaced by a panorama of marsh and water, distant points and islands, and framed by a yet more distant horizon of wooded uplands. You have clearly entered something more than a wide place in the river.

But if you start at the head of tide on the Kennebec or the Androscoggin, which widen gradually as they approach their convergence, the precise point at which you enter the Bay is less distinct. This is especially true of the Kennebec. Some maps put the line of demarcation as far south as Brown's Point, in easternmost Bowdoinham, thus depriving Richmond, Dresden, and poor Perkins of any claim to bay frontage. Most people I know, including all of the ones who have spent their whole lives knocking around on the Bay, put the northern boundary well upstream from there, usually at the Richmond-Dresden bridge, which is an admittedly artificial line of demarcation. Maine's Department of Game and Inland Fisheries defines the Bay as the area between the Chops and the first upstream bridge on each of the rivers

The Chops, opening into the Bay. Sturgeon Island is on the right.

flowing into it. That does well enough as a working definition, although I tend to think of Merrymeeting Bay in terms of its most conspicuous and characteristic crop, wild rice, and so to include in it the whole of the tidal portions of the Abby, Cathance, Muddy, and Eastern and several miles of the Kennebec above the Richmond bridge.

Within this area, the mean tidal range varies from not quite six feet to a little less than four, and the tides run from two to three hours behind those at the mouth of the river. The deepest water in the Bay is at the Chops itself, and a fine channel runs northward along the Woolwich–Dresden shore from there on up to Richmond and beyond. The Androscoggin channel was never as deep, but two hundred years ago, it was easily navigable by small coastal schooners all the way up to the head of tide in Brunswick. The combined results of upstream damming and soil erosion had badly reduced its flow by the middle of the nineteenth century, and it is now easily navigable only by hovercraft. I have a less appropriate vessel, and in trying to make my way at low tide from the Bay up toward Brunswick, I have churned a great deal of sand, done considerable wading, and come close to concluding that the Androscoggin channel is an erroneous navigational hypothesis, like the Northwest Passage, where the expedition of an earlier Franklin came to grief. But I am repeatedly assured by unimpeachable authorities that such a channel does in fact exist, winding through the Saharan shallows between Pleasant Point in Topsham and Butler Head in Bath.

What is true of the Androscoggin mouth is also true of the mouths of the Muddy, the Cathance, the Abby, and the Eastern. Each forms its own delta within the larger delta of the Bay, creating an extensive intertidal zone of mudflats, sandbars, and marshes, veined by small channels, creeks, and guzzles. At dead low tide, nearly half of the total area of the Bay is out of the water, and most of the rest of it is shallow—less than ten feet deep. A beautiful beach, the Sands, emerges for a couple of hours a day smack in the middle of the Bay, directly opposite the Chops.

Because it has so little deepwater frontage, there are no public landings directly on the Bay, and nothing remains of anything resembling a working waterfront—no icehouses, boatyards, or wharves. If you look closely along the shore, you can find rotting, overgrown pilings and abutments, and be able to recognize, here and there, that what now resembles a natural formation was once a mole or breakwater. The wild rice stirs and sighs in the wind; the surrounding uplands present a vision of New England pastoral, giving an illusion of timelessness and completion: pastures, woodlots, frame houses. In contemporary Boston or New York, you must deliberately remind yourself that you are in a place that was once a modest human settlement in the middle of big marshes and rivers that swarmed with life. On the Bay, it's the other way around—you must remind yourself that a century and a half ago, this was a busy scene: logs being shepherded down from the interior, boomed up when the tide turned; schooners built in Richmond, Bowdoinham, or Perkins making their way seaward; scows and barges maintaining a commerce that connected a dozen or so towns and communities. In winter, teams of men and horses were busy strip-mining the frozen river, cutting ice by the ton and storing it in huge riverside warehouses. In spring and summer, drift netters, weir minders, and sturgeon fishermen occupied the foreground, and in the background, at all seasons of the year, plumes of smoke and steam rose from shipyards and sawmills. There would have been very few woodlots or even trees in sight: wood was what heated houses and generated steam power, and land, even very poor land, was for pasture, orchards, and crops.

So if you sit in your boat in the middle of the Bay on a sweet late summer morning, your sense will be of a surprising solitude and of lovely, modulated distances, and your pleasure in that will be augmented by the old pleasure, which must be rooted in our hunter-gatherer heritage, of being surrounded by life, seen and unseen. Human and natural history appear to have settled into a peaceful co-existence. In fact they have not—not here, and not anywhere else on earth. Part of your mind knows that, and it is important not to ignore what you know. But it is also important to see what is, at and for the present moment, in front of your eyes.

Revenant

THERE ARE THE REGULAR EVENTS OF THE CLOCK and the calendar, the fiscal year, the baseball season, the electoral cycle, and so forth, and then there are other events that punctuate time, dividing personal or local or larger histories into a Before and an After. There was the late-summer day when the levees north of New Orleans gave way; there was the day a child was born or an old dog died.

In the thirty-seven years since I first saw Merrymeeting Bay, spring, summer, fall, and winter have come and gone with their usual variations and irregularities, some of them dramatic. There have been ten presidential elections, thirty-seven World Series, and something more than 26,350 ebbings and flowings of the tide. The United States has concluded the Vietnam War, the first incontrovertible military defeat in its history. The Four Horsemen of the Apocalypse—war, famine, pestilence, and death—have ridden roughshod over Africa, and still do. Cambodia has endured the genocidal campaign of a revolutionary government against its people, murder on a scale not seen since the end of World War II.

The Soviet Union has invaded Afghanistan and met

ferocious Islamic opposition, a lot of it encouraged and sustained by the United States. Its defeat has much to do with the end of its empire and of the Cold War. These events led the historian Francis Fukuyama to proclaim the end of history itself, the final triumph of the good guys—people who believed first and foremost in democracy, free trade, capitalism, and tolerance, and only secondarily and more or less recreationally in anything else. He was, of course, dead wrong. The American mainland, inviolate through two world wars and the whole of the Cold War, has been attacked, and we have a new war on our hands, against an enemy having no fixed address, no homeland, and no visible army. In practice, we have waged the new war in the old way, invading countries, gaining clear-cut victories over whatever organized military resistance we encountered, and yet coming no closer to anything that could be called victory.

These anxieties and calamities have distracted our attention from ominous changes in Nature itself. The world is indisputably growing warmer, and at a rate that has exceeded even the most pessimistic forecasts of twenty or twenty-five years ago. Hurricanes have greatly increased in their intensity and duration. Mount Kilimanjaro in Tanzania has lost 80 percent of its famous snow; glaciers have receded and permafrost has thawed. In a matter of a few weeks, a chunk of the Antarctic ice shelf the size of Rhode Island fell into the sea. It had been there since the end of the last Ice Age, twelve thousand years ago, when Bowdoinham lay beneath an arctic sea.

In the immediate, three-dimensional reality of Bowdoinham, the spring of 1987 saw the greatest flooding of the Kennebec and the Androscoggin on record. To get to work, I had to drive south to Topsham, then north to I-95, then south to Freeport, then north, finally, to Brunswick. Eleven years later we had the biggest ice storm in anybody's memory, and cooked and heated with wood, read by candlelight, hauled water in buckets, and found that Nostalgia is not a bad place to visit, but you wouldn't want to live there.

Things changed on the Bay, too, and in at least two cases it was very much for the better. The implementation of the Clean Rivers Act in 1977 enormously increased the numbers of fish—alewives, stripers, sturgeon—that one saw there. The Androscoggin, which used to blister and discolor the paint on riverside buildings in Lewiston, no longer churned itself into a hideous lather as it fell down to tidewater in Brunswick. Cormorants, eagles, osprey, herons, and mergansers benefitted, and there began to be some hope for the restoration of the shad runs still remembered by old-timers, and even for the return of Atlantic salmon.

All of these hopes were enlarged by the removal of the Edwards Dam on the Kennebec in 1999, which re-opened for spawning a section of the river that had been blockaded since 1837. Slowly and incompletely, the Kennebec and the

Androscoggin are being gentrified: once blue collar rivers, valued only insofar as they served the purposes of industry, they are being refurbished as something suited to the economy of tourism and outdoor recreation that seeks to replace the old one of mills and mill towns.

Other changes are less explicable. For as long as anyone can remember, the great harbingers of spring in Bowdoinham and the other towns around the Bay were Canada geese. They always began showing up around the traditional date for town meeting—March 20; it was something people commented on, and liked. In April you could drive around the Bay and see hundreds of them, grazing or simply standing in fields, and you could hear their clamorous, urgent braying from the Bay whenever the wind was right. Flying low on overcast days, with the fields still frozen and ponds and puddles glazed with ice, they seemed tough, vital, and thrillingly wild, an antidote and a challenge to the lethargy and despair of indoor existence. They now seem to have reconsidered their ways and opted for gentrification themselves—for life in city parks and suburbs, on exclusive golf courses and the landscaped lawns of corporate headquarters. In a typical spring now, I see only a few hundred, where I used to see thousands, and can work outdoors all day in April and never hear a single honk.

Blue-winged teal, compared to green-wings, and black ducks, compared to mallards, have both decreased signifi-cantly on the Bay. In the case of black ducks, this simply reflects a North American trend that has been steadily downward, although that does not explain why mallards, distinctly uncommon on the Bay thirty years ago, have now become so prevalent there. As for the blue-winged teal—an exceptionally handsome little bird—its decline seems to be more local and anomalous, and, except among duck hunters, not much commented upon.

A DIFFERENT KIND OF EVENT, inviting a different way of thinking about time and history, occurred in the late winter and early spring of 1997, when, in the first hours of darkness, the Hale-Bopp comet streamed fuzzily and placidly across our northwest sky, and reappeared in the northeast shortly before dawn. In our astronomical ignorance, my wife and I resemble most citizens of developed and artificially illuminated nations, and we first saw the comet before we had read or heard anything about it. We were taking our usual after supper walk and there it was, a soft neon glow fairly low in the sky over the village. It was nothing like the stars that glittered coldly and remotely overhead; more like a small moon, seen through a mist.

Once we found out what it was, we quickly got accustomed to it. Its blurred incandescence was a welcome contrast to the hard, skeletal outlines of winter—bare trees against the horizon, the lights from houses illuminating yards

The Chops at dawn, late winter

that looked like frozen puddles. It would not have been half so impressive or so welcome in a summer sky. When it passed on into the vast outer darkness of its orbit, we knew that we would miss it.

We learned that it had last come this way about 4,200 years ago, and would not return for another couple of thousand years. I tried to imagine what this region would have been like the last time it swung by, and who the inhabitants were, and what they would have made of it. That was virtually impossible, but it was a lot easier, and on the whole more comforting, than in trying to imagine who would live here, or whether Bowdoinham, or even the Bay itself would be here at all, on its next visit. Four thousand years ago was before any history that I knew anything about. Two thousand years hence, judging from the political and meteorological events of the past three or four decades, is a vaster unknown than the origins or outermost reaches of the cosmos.

Sometimes our evening walk took us as far as the bridge over the Cathance, where Jimmy McPherson has his smelt camps. He had gotten them on the ice late that year, and had pulled them off early—it had been a poor winter for enterprises requiring thick ice or deep snow. His cheerful little village—one street of shacks, each shack spaced ten or twelve feet from its neighbor, illuminated by a single light bulb, and, when business was booming, huffing and puffing

woodsmoke like a Mississippi River steamboat—had been granted a historical existence of seventeen days in the winter of 1996–97. Even during that span, he and his crew had to re-position the camps, because the ice had shifted gradually downstream, moving them perilously close to the open water underneath the bridge. There were other complications as well—on a busy night, with each of the two dozen or so camps full, there were fifteen or twenty tons of weight on the ice. With the ice less dense than usual, the rising tide, instead of lifting the entire village, sometimes forced itself up through seams and fissures in the ice, spread across its surface, and caused, insofar as smeltville was concerned, severe local flooding and an emergency evacuation. I asked Jimmy if he had a siren or any other way to warn his clients of the danger. "Nah," he said. "They figure it out for themselves, once the water hits the stove and she starts to sizzle. Most of 'em, anyways."

I could have thought to myself that Jimmy's operation was human and even geological history writ small: the establishment of human settlements, their apparently solid and durable reality, their sudden passing. The rising and subsiding of sea levels, the advance or retreat of glaciers, and the massive shifting, in microscopic increments, of tectonic plates, dividing continents and hemispheres from each other. But why think such a thing? By the time the comet had faded from our sight, spring was well on the way—killdeers showing up and peepers hard at it. Sooner than had seemed possible in February, it would be May, the busiest season of the year, and there was no time for long-term philosophizing.

But now, almost a decade later, I find myself not so much thinking about Hale-Bopp as simply wanting to see it again, and recapture the strange aura that seemed to enclose us when Susan and I walked out on those cold evenings, talking about and noticing perfectly ordinary things in perfectly ordinary ways. It gave a ghostliness to those things, reminding us, I suppose, of the ephemerality of everything that we assume is real, when seen against the immensities of time and space that frame our lives.

Transcience and Evidence

THE MELTING ICECAP RECEDED, leaving ocean behind. Thirteen thousand years ago, the Kennebec River did not exist. If it had, its head of tide would have been somewhere in the vicinity of Bingham, with a glacier looming over it. Bowdoinham and the Bay lay deep below the surface of an iceberg-littered sea, and upland Maine was one solid mass of ice. The warming continued, the earth, compressed by all that weight of ice, rebounded, and Merrymeeting Bay first took shape as the place where, within a few miles of each other, two youthful rivers, both fed by the glacial meltwater from north-central and northwestern Maine, came down to the sea. The land continued to rise; the headlands that flank the Chops went from being insular to being continental, and the river mouth kept moving south—further south, in fact, than it is today. By ten thousand years ago, the local geography had assumed something like its present shape, although the coastline would have been substantially further out than it is now. Continued glacial melting raised ocean levels again, although not so drastically as before, and gave Maine's many islands, peninsulas, and ledges their contemporary—and no doubt temporary—coordinates.

Vegetation spread north on the heels of the glacier. It was followed by animals, and they were followed by people. The first of them—hunters of muskox, bison, caribou, mastodon, mammoth, and an extinct species of horse—have left evidence of themselves from between ten and eleven thousand years ago. They first roamed a largely treeless landscape, then one with a scattering of stunted trees and a general resemblance to Labrador.

I have on more than one occasion dutifully attempted to take this chronology in, and to make the leap of faith that ignorance must always make, if it is ever to get past square one. To that end, I sat on the porch of a friend, whom I'll call Tobin, over in east Bowdoinham on a fine September afternoon. Beyond the field in front of us, we could see the mouth of the Abby, where now and again a small gang of teal got up out of the marshes, flew a short distance, and settled back down. As always at that season, there were harriers about, canting and tilting just above the tips of the rice, and no doubt keeping the teal at a fine pitch of anxiety. We talked for a while, then Tobin went inside and brought out a small, handsome wooden box. He did not handle it casually. Inside it were evidences of the deep human past of this vicinity.

He is not an archeologist, and had only done what any observant person might do—working in his garden, he had noticed a shard of stone that looked a little odd and had a suggestion of symmetry about it. Because he is human, he was curious, and because he is a civilized, reflective man, he took his curiosity seriously. He no longer stumbles upon things by chance. Now he walks around Bowdoinham and the Bay with his head down, and a sense of where to look. If the place is especially likely, he may get down on all fours and nose around like a raccoon, trying to discover some one fragment that was not shaped by geology among the many that were.

And so he showed me his collection, and talked about the cultures it represented—the Paleo-Indians, who were replaced by or mutated into the Red Paint people, who three thousand years ago, at about the time King David was ascending to the throne of Israel, themselves gave way to or became the Ceramic people. These last were the nations—Micmac, Abenaki, Passamaquoddy, and so forth—that the first Europeans found here. We therefore have some account of their lives and customs, although that account is always inflected by the fear, longing, greed, self-justification, ideological convenience, theological conviction, guilt, and nostalgia of the Euro-Americans who pushed them violently into the deep, inaccessible vault of the past.

I do not believe that either of us was entirely free of guilt, longing, or nostalgia as we looked at the contents of the box. I would have recognized perhaps a quarter of them as human handiwork. The majority of the pieces had no

Friends of Merrymeeting Bay annual Bay Day for local children. Two future marine biologists examine a seine; a future archaeologist sifts the evidence.

3,000-year-old hearth, Mugford Site, Topsham

identifying shape. They were flat, like skipping stones or fragments of an oyster shell. Their perimeters were unevenly and rather randomly scalloped. You had to look closely and to know what you were looking for to see that their edges resulted from an angled flecking and chipping—a human hand, using another stone or perhaps the tine of an antler, tapping carefully. The ragged, irregular tool that resulted would not have been nearly so good for cutting or scraping as a knife is, but it represented a crucial improvement over teeth or fingernails.

The more obviously shaped pieces were arrowheads and spearpoints, some perfect, some broken. Many of the other pieces—perhaps most of them—must have represented partial failures: arrowheads that did not work out, but could still be used to worry the flesh off a hide, or haggle open the belly of a sturgeon. Tobin said that the work of the Paleo-Indians was particularly fastidious, seldom equaled by their successors in Maine, or by Stone Age people anywhere on earth.

And he said that he sometimes closes his eyes, here or there around the Bay, and imagines a steady, insect-like clicking and chipping filling the air around him—all those people, all those years, leaving their very modest, very durable detritus. They used chert, slate, quartz, and rhyolite, and found very little of it locally. Some of the stone came from elsewhere in Maine; some, to my astonishment, from as far away as Pennsylvania, Nova Scotia, or central New York State. Their total numbers were never great—one book estimates about 32,000 people were living in the whole extent of what is now Maine and the Maritime Provinces when the Europeans arrived. But they obviously had networks of communication and commerce, even as far back as the Paleo-Indian era, upon which they depended for the stone that was no less essential to their survival than fish, birds, mammals, and fire.

The most beautiful thing in the box was a stone gouge. On it, you could see traces of red pigment—it had been placed in a man's grave, because the dead were assumed to have a future. And possibly this man did, in some other realm of being; but his people did not. The grave itself somehow disappeared under the centuries and millennia of rain, decay, frost heaves, erosion, and all the other minute, incessant processes by which landscapes go on shaping themselves. The gouge was half embedded in a bank; Tobin was paddling by and it caught his well-trained attention. When he picked it up, he picked up something older than the language we were speaking or the languages that were its parents and grandparents. About all that was the same between its time and ours was the human hand—the one that had made it and the one that now, our conversation complete, carefully put the gouge back into its box and closed the lid.

Short-nosed sturgeon

An Intimation of Immortality

Unless you are very young, ten thousand years ago, when the human history of the Bay began, is not an inconceivable span of time. If you've been around for fifty years or so, the idea of a century has become quite manageable for you; it is your life plus one other life. Only two hundred such lives separate this May morning from one dawning upon the subarctic landscape of paleolithic Bowdoinham. The landscape itself isn't inconceivable either—we can get a reasonable idea of it by going to the contemporary North American subarctic.

In May, amid all the excitement of emerging leaves, sprouting seeds, and returning birds, sturgeon begin nosing their way upstream, bent on spawning. They've had this habit for a long time, and quite recently it has run them head on into an invasive species that has established itself throughout their range—us. And we have had the habit of catching them for what we would consider a long time, too—in fact, for almost all of our history as a North American species. Huge, slow, toothless, and unarmored, they made for easy pickings whenever they came up into narrow or shallow water, or congregated at the foot of a waterfall. They were not programmed to take notice of us and the threat we pose.

When the Europeans arrived, they found the Bay full of sturgeon and immediately began exploiting them. The first commercial fishery in North America was established at the head of tide on the Androscoggin in 1628. Sturgeon were also the first cash crop to be harvested in Jamestown, Virginia. In both places, the fish were cured and shipped back to England, where their flesh was considered a delicacy and said to resemble veal. The tough skin was worked into a kind of leather—books were bound in it—and the membrane of the air bladder, when properly cleaned, yielded a substance called isinglass, which was used to clarify wine and beer.

Here in Maine and all across North America, Euro-Americans netted, trapped, and speared sturgeon without restraint; they built weirs, dams, and mills that cut off and contaminated most of their spawning grounds. Once there were too few of them to be commercially significant, we simply forgot them. Sportsmen did not rush to their defense, as they did for stripers, salmon, and shad. Nor, more surprisingly, did commercial fishermen. Nor, until very recently, did even environmentalists, and thus far they have not been able to stir much sympathy for this odd and antiquated fish.

This is how locally neglected they have been. Until 1970, when research was being done on the ecology of Montsweag Bay, over in Wiscasset, nobody seems to have realized that we had two distinct species of sturgeon in the state—the short-nosed and the Atlantic. Prior to that, adult short-noses were assumed to be immature Atlantic sturgeon. Ten years later, Peter Thompson's attractive book, *The Game Fishes of New England and South Eastern Canada*, listed the Atlantic Sturgeon and the Lake Sturgeon (which inhabits the Great Lakes and the Saint Lawrence watershed), but failed to mention their short-nosed cousin. And yet the short-nose is by far the more common species in Maine. Misidentification and general ignorance have benefitted the short-nose, making it seem more severely threatened than it is and earning it the status of an endangered species. It was the other way around for the Atlantic. When a few big adult Atlantic sturgeon began reappearing in the Kennebec in the late 1970s, the state permitted them to be harvested commercially. In the first year, 1980, thirty-two adult fish were caught. In the next year, none. None again the year after that. Three in 1983, after which the Department of Marine Resources reinstated the ban on harvesting them.

Where I grew up in coastal South Carolina, members of my father's generation could remember one or two occasions when a shad fisherman had accidentally caught a big Atlantic sturgeon in his nets and gotten his picture in the paper. But I had never seen one at all. Their disappearance had for me no special pathos or significance, although I was the kind of little boy who got pretty worked up over other extinct or gravely threatened species, like the Carolina parakeet or the whooping crane. Until I got to Bowdoinham, I, like most people in this country, thought of sturgeon as a source of caviar, if I thought of them at all.

It IS BECAUSE OF CAVIAR that sturgeon have been most prized, and are now most threatened, in that part of the world known as the Aralo-Caspian Depression—a formerly submerged area between the Baltic and the Black Sea, extending as far eastward as the Caspian Sea. Six of the world's twenty-six or twenty-seven species (it seems to depend on who is counting) live there, including *Acipenser sturio*, the one we call the Atlantic sturgeon, and also including *Acipenser huso*, or beluga sturgeon. The beluga (the name means *white*, as also in the beluga whale) is the largest of its tribe, and may weigh more than a ton. One that size would be a female; when spawning, she would carry better than two hundred pounds of roe. It has long been valued above all other sturgeon roe by people living in the vicinity of the Black and Caspian Seas and along the big rivers—the Volga, the Danube—that feed into them. When pickled in brine, beluga roe is generally considered the caviar of all caviars.

The taste for caviar gradually migrated westward. By about 1500, a few western Europeans had realized that it is to fish eggs as champagne is to vinegar. In 1601 Shakespeare had Hamlet speak of an excellent play that was not a crowd-pleaser as being "caviare to the general"—that is, pearls before swine when it came to ordinary folk like you and me. It still retains its social and gustatorial cachet, having become the debutante's Dorito, the plutocrat's potato chip.

The czars and upper Russian aristocracy were devoted to caviar, and the commissars and *apparatchiki* who replaced them were careful to preserve this vestige of privilege and autocracy, because it was a reliable source of good, hard, cold, decadent capitalist cash. During the Soviet period, beluga sturgeon were managed carefully, and the penalties for poaching or black-marketing caviar were savage. The collapse of the Soviet Union put an end to that—the market and the resource are now controlled by the Russian mafia, and it is estimated that the beluga population has declined by at least 90 percent since 1970. The species may not last another decade, as there seems to be neither the will nor the resources to protect it.

The taste for caviar, and a realization of its cash value, reached this country late in the nineteenth century. In the years leading up to the First World War, America provided something like 90 percent of the world's caviar, shipping most of it to Europe, where it was generally sold as Russian caviar, and sometimes imported back into the United States under that alien alias, which greatly increased its market value. Overfishing thus combined with the damming of rivers and destruction of spawning habitat to put the various species of North American sturgeon in the rare and endangered category.

Locally, it is estimated that between seven and ten thousand short-nosed sturgeon inhabit the Bay and the lower Kennebec. There do not seem to be any firm estimates for Atlantic sturgeon—their numbers are certainly much lower, although evidence suggests that the population may be rebounding, undoubtedly helped by the removal of the Edwards Dam, which has granted them access to prime spawning waters. We know that a female short-nose is about ten years old before she spawns for the first time, and that she goes at least three years between spawnings. The Atlantic is substantially slower to reach sexual maturity, and probably spawns less frequently. We know that the short-noses that spawn in the Kennebec are genetically distinct from those that spawn in the Androscoggin. We know that the young sturgeon ride back and forth with the tide, keeping within a moving zone of brackish waters. We know that the adults eat, among many other things, zebra mussels, an invasive species we could do without.

Consider what such meager knowledge has as its object. Sturgeon date from a past and a planet that we cannot conceive of by any analogy or extrapolation from our own experience. Ten thousand years are as nothing to them. Fossil sturgeon, very similar in all respects to *Acipenser sturio*, indicate that the species was thriving during the Cretaceous Period, seventy to a hundred million years ago. As you no doubt recall, the Cretaceous was eventful and stressful; such imposing creatures as dinosaurs flourished in it and ultimately succumbed to it. It is hard to see what design features allowed the sturgeon to swim unscathed through that massive biocide. It is a fish—unhurried, benthic, fond of big rivers—that is older than the Andes Mountains and that, having changed a lot less than they have, swims past our backyards every spring. It has seen continents drift, lived and thrived and left its fossilized remains in sea basins that are now dry land, observed the advance and retreat of glaciers, the depression and rebounding of the earth's surface, the first mammals, the first humanoids, the first jet-skis. The slow motion apocalypses of geology and evolution have passed over it, signifying less to it than the turnings of the tide and the cycle of the seasons. By our standards sturgeon have no conception of time—almost no *experience* of it. By their standards we are bubbles on the stream.

They look strange, as though cobbled together out of zoological spare parts. The tapering snout and small eyes, set well back in the head, give them a facial resemblance to an ordinary garden mole. The bony plates, or scutes, along the back and sides are vaguely alligatorish. The scimitar-shaped tail is borrowed from a shark. The lips, on the underside of the snout, are protrusile, like those of human beings and

Cabbassa—Atlantic sturgeon

chimpanzees, only much more so. Between the mouth and the tip of the nose is a stiff, rudimentary moustache of tactile barbels. When the barbels detect something edible in the mud, the lips protrude and smooch, inhale and ingest. The tail flexes and the creature moves on—a submersible, self-propelled vacuum cleaner.

From time to time they jump, for no apparent reason. Thirty-five years ago, more or less, I was out on the Sands and saw a silvery, cylindrical fish jump. It was a long way off. I felt sure it was a salmon—a misconception begotten by Hope upon Ignorance. It was a short-nosed sturgeon, as anybody who had spent any time on the Bay or lower Kennebec could have told me. They are a common enough sight, and sometimes land themselves in somebody's boat, although I am still waiting for that to happen to me. It is much less common, and much more memorable, to see a mature Atlantic sturgeon go airborne. They jump in the same fashion that the short-noses do, coming completely out of the water with their snouts pointed toward the heavens like a Polaris missle launched from a submarine, then falling back in, tail first. Once, on a calm day, I saw a biggish one—I estimated him to be about the size of a professional basketball player—jump a long way off, and saw the big splash he made, then heard it, a massive, watery thud.

The first people around the Bay undoubtedly valued the fish, and for more than as a source of protein. Something that big must have conveyed an inference of divinity. A brave walked down to the Kennebec, near Gardiner. It was spring. He said, "I am a sturgeon," and jumped into the river. Uncomprehending and full of woe, his family and friends, all the people of his tribe, rushed to the edge of the water and called his name. He did not re-appear, but a huge sturgeon rolled out in the channel. From that time forward, the people of his tribe called themselves after the Abenaki word for sturgeon—*cabbassa*. When asked to identify themselves, they quoted the last words of the doomed brave: I am a sturgeon. Cobbossee Stream, dumping into the Kennebec in Gardiner, derives its name from cabbassa; Cobbosseecontee Lake, which the stream drains, comes from cabbassaguntiquoke—a place where sturgeon are found.

Later people around the Bay, not familiar with its largest and oldest inhabitant, may react differently. One pleasant evening a few summers ago, Peter Coviello, a youngish scholar of nineteenth-century American Literature and a colleague of mine in the English Department at Bowdoin, sat with friends on the deck of the Sea Dog Pub in Topsham. Twenty feet below the deck is the Androscoggin; fifty yards upstream are the falls at the head of the tide. It is a very pleasant place late on a summer afternoon, with the deck catching the sun, the ledges on the Brunswick side deep in shadow, and the dark, still waters of the Androscoggin down below.

Dark, still waters suggest a deep, abiding placidity; alternatively, they suggest the possibility of something lurking. As a student of nineteenth-century American literature, Peter was not unaware of the contradictory possibilities of the scene before him, but, as a decent, human man, he was rather more aware of the pleasures of a moment of civilized ease and conversation, both things greatly enhanced by a beer or two. His vocation has provided him with many vicarious encounters with Nature. Monsters of the deep—Moby Dick, Hemingway's marlin, or the mighty sturgeon Nahma that leaps from the waters of Gitchee Gumee to swallow Hiawatha, light canoe and all, in Longfellow's long, long poem—hold no terrors for him. Not on paper they don't. But it would have to be said that closer encounters of the natural kind make him uneasy. At a formative age, he saw a seriously bad movie about a psychopathic white shark, and it unsettled him permanently when it comes to beaches, boats, deep water, and large fish.

You can see where this is going. He told me about it later, still a little discombobulated. A sturgeon jumped in the river, right there in front of him. Nothing unusual about this: sturgeon have occasionally jumped there for as long as the Androscoggin River has been in business. I questioned Peter closely.

"About a yard long?"

"No. Big. I mean BIG"—eyes wide, a look of residual

Atlantic sturgeon

Short-nosed sturgeon

horror and hyperbolic sincerity.

"Maybe he just LOOKED big. He surprised you; you'd had a beer or two."

"This was not the first occasion upon which I have had a beer or two," he said, with a formal and somewhat starchy dignity, "nor was it indeed the very first time something untoward has befallen me in that circumstance. *I tell you, I am talking about a freaking fish the size of me or you.*"

In the end, he persuaded me. He had not seen a short-nose. He had seen an Atlantic sturgeon. I congratulated him, and envied him, too. I told him all about the fish's great antiquity, speculated that Longfellow himself had possibly seen Atlantic sturgeon jump at this very spot, back when he was an undergraduate at Bowdoin, and assured him that the fish were utterly harmless, although they grew to sizes much greater than he or I or Shaquille O'Neal, for that matter. To see one like that might be regarded as an honor, an omen.

Perhaps he should undertake to write about *The Song of Hiawatha*. I am obliged to say that all of this was, like so many other lectures, caviare to the general, water off a duck's back. By and large, people do not appreciate being told that their phobias are irrational.

But Peter still patronizes the Sea Dog, perhaps on the theory that lightning does not strike twice in the same place. Or perhaps on the theory that you must confront your fears. And certainly on the theory that, on a pleasant summer evening, there above the smoothly gliding Androscoggin, a civilized and reflective man, equipped with a beer, could do a lot worse than to sit and converse with friends inside, while the Yankees play the Red Sox on the big TV set above the bar, and no one risks being reminded of what holy prehistoric horrors—dark, log-shaped, log-sized bodies, with the slow power and persistence of continents—may be nuzzling their way upstream.

OLD-TIMERS REMEMBER FISH WEIRS on the tide flats. Linwood Rideout has described them to me: stakes driven into the mud, gray birch saplings woven in between them to make a kind of fence, running perpendicular to the shore. When fish moving along the shore on the ebb tide encountered the fence, they would follow it outward, apparently toward deeper water and freedom. But at its outer end the fence circled inward. "Like a roll of snow fence, when it's not all the way unrolled," Linwood said. Once inside the inner circle of the fence, the fish swam round and round, never reversing direction and so never finding their way out.

Gray birch—they called it old field birch, because it was often the first thing to come into a rocky upland field if you stopped mowing it—was the best thing for weaving between the weir stakes because of its dense, crooked, twiggy crown. In the weir at low tide they found alewives and stripers and such, but shad were the primary target.

Shad ran when the shadbush bloomed. So you had to have your weir all built and ready by then. But it was more usual to catch them with drift nets, generally deployed at night. The shad were skittish, and would avoid the mesh in daylight. You wanted to handle the boat with minimum commotion, for the same reason. But the shad were worth the trouble. During the Great Depression, when cash was short, you could trade them at the Bowdoinham store for

The Oldest Profession

sugar, meat, flour, or whatever else you were running short of; the store would put out a sign advertising fresh shad, and they'd go in a hurry, because shad were already becoming a local rarity.

But if it was eels you were after, you either gigged or set traps for them—the traps look something like a cross between a lobster trap and an ordinary minnow trap. In the years I've been here, there have been two boom times for the eel fishery. In the 1970s, a Scandinavian market opened up, and a number of local men of more or less my own generation added eel fishing to their generally extensive list of seasonal vocations, which might or might not be combined with a more or less regular job. From time to time you would see a small tank truck at the town landing, and Bruce Berry or Joe Trafton or Jimmy McPherson there in a big, flat-bottomed skiff, off-loading a writhing, slithering cargo. The eels were shipped live across the Atlantic. They are tough customers, able to survive for a long time if they are kept cool and damp. By the late 1970s, the uncertainties of demand and supply had taken their toll, and this small revival of a commercial fishery on the Bay went into decline, although it did not die out entirely. Then in the 1990s, a new market opened in Asia. This time, the customers were interested not only in the adult eels, but also in elvers—tiny little fellows that are spawned in the Sargasso Sea, east of Bermuda, and

drift on the Gulf Stream for a year or more, and then, at a mysteriously predetermined moment, some of them become capable of self-propulsion and wriggle their way inshore, up our rivers and brooks. Others continue to drift for another year or two, and wind up in Europe. The process is apparently as involuntary and infallible as the upward growth of an oak toward the sun, or the downward fall of its acorn toward the earth.

Jimmy McPherson, who manages to find something that keeps him remuneratively busy on the Bay in every season of the year, and in that respect is, as far as I know, the last of a distinctive local breed, still traps eels, although he is not sanguine about the future. His business is complex and uncertain; its variables are global. The eels he ships to Asia are scarcely bigger than a blade of grass when they come in from the wide salt sea, and they must run a gauntlet of gulls, terns, fish, and fyke nets to reach the waters where they will grow to maturity and live out their adult lives. His preferred bait, horseshoe crab, is shipped up from the southern and mid-Atlantic coasts. The rapid development of the southern conch fishery, which also prizes the crabs for bait, has in recent years driven their price sharply upward, reducing the margins within which he operates.

When Jimmy goes out of his business—it is, like most things on this earth, only a matter of time—and if, as seems likely, nobody else goes into it, that will mark the end of our most ancient local enterprise. Alder Stream empties into Sebasticook Lake empties into the Sebasticook River empties into the Kennebec, up near Waterville. In 1991 remains of an eel weir were found near the mouth of the stream and the stakes were carbon-dated. The oldest ones had been driven into the mud about 5,800 years ago, and the newest ones about forty or forty-one centuries later. That is a lot of years of doing business in one location. Euro-Americans continued the tradition further downstream—references from the eighteenth century designate a rapid on the lower Sebasticook as Eel Weir Rips. One of the very last eel weirs in Maine is on Twentyfive Mile Stream, another tributary of the Sebasticook—Heather Perry's photographs of adult silver eels, captured on their way downriver toward the Sargasso, come from there. Both the indigenous people and the colonists who replaced them gigged eels through the ice up and down the Kennebec and its tributaries—gigs from the last century, which look something like a smaller version of a yard rake and were designed to pinch the eels between the tines rather than to impale them, still show up from time to time in antique catalogues and auction barns. As fish go, eels are exceptionally nourishing—a rich, fatty food that was prized for as long as undernourishment, rather than overnourishment, was a chronic hazard to North American health.

But it takes a good deal of education to develop an enthusiasm for eels—sturgeon, carp, and catfish are charismatic by comparison. If, with no other motive but an idle and untutored curiosity, you should decide to pull up an eel pot, as Susan and I once did on the Cathance, back in the 1970s, you may find in it what we found—a moiling, slithering mass, more wormlike than fishlike, of dusky green to dusky brown heads and bodies, weaving in and out. They look obscene, like the innards of something, or the murky contents of a childhood nightmare. They don't hiss, but you keep expecting them to. You may be inspired, as we were, to drop the pot back into the water pronto. Prior to that, my encounters with eels had been inadvertent—occasionally catching one while fishing for flounder back in South Carolina, or collecting a minnow trap and finding no minnows in it, but only a single sluggish and bulging eel.

It is hard to believe that such a creature could ever be endangered—I am ashamed to say that in my private scheme of vertebrate and invertebrate classification, I used to put them somewhere between rats and cockroaches as members of the Ancient and Eternal Order of Indestructible Vermin. You find them in unlikely places—under a damp rock at the edge of a stream, or in a tiny runnel of water, not deep enough to cover their backs, in a low-lying pasture. They could, you feel, insinuate themselves into the most private recesses of your life, psychologically if not, you hope, literally.

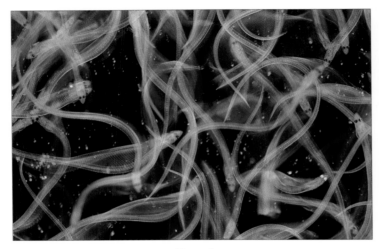

Glass eels

Juvenile eels, called yellow eels

Yellow eels, at this point 8–10 inches long and the diameter of a pencil

Yellow eels ascending a dam to reach Sebasticook Stream

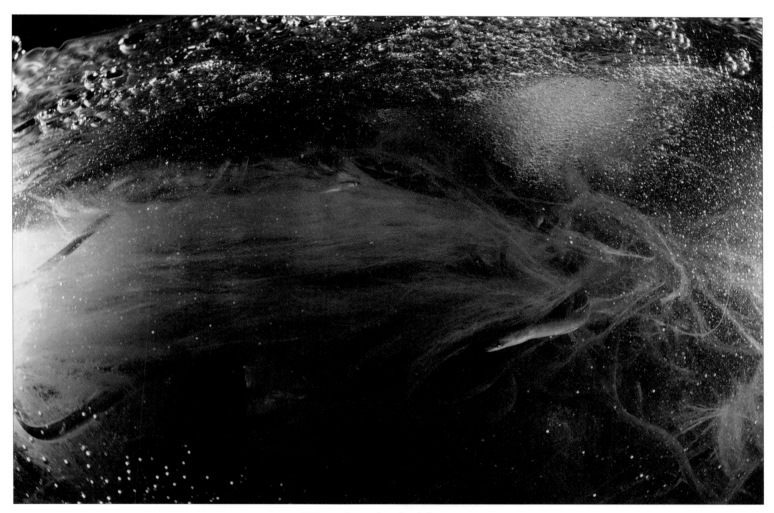

Yellow eels in algae, headed upstream

A mature female silver eel setting out on her first and last return trip to the Sargasso Sea

Silver eel

Glass eels, just in from the sea and still transparent

And yet, tough as they are, adaptable as they are, enterprising as they are, uncuddlesome as they are, they are in a lot of trouble. They live a long time in fresh water—a decade or two or three or even more—growing, thickening, eating about everything and being eaten by a great many things—cormorants and stripers, to name two of their more conspicuous local predators—and taking no care for posterity. Then, after having passed whole decades in the rivers, they respond to internal or external changes we cannot understand, and strike out for the Sargasso. It always happens in the fall, usually October. When they get back there to where they started, they spawn and die, betting all those years of survival on one roll of the dice. It is at the beginning of this great terminal migration that they are most vulnerable. The weir at Alder Stream six millennia ago was a V-shaped funnel, pointing downstream, and so is the one still in operation on Twenty-five Mile Stream. A basket is placed at the end of the funnel. In theory, every eel that comes down the stream enters the funnel and ends up in the basket.

But the eel population withstood eel weirs, gigs, eel pots, stripers, gulls, and so forth. Although their movement upriver and access to the full range of available habitat has been impeded by dams, the effect of this has been less severe than with anadromous fish, because it has not cut them off from their spawning grounds, and also because when journeying upriver they are small enough and persistent enough to get over, around, or through dams that would stop ordinary fish. But when the full-grown females head downstream, it is a different story. They are drawn into the millrace and mangled by the blades of the turbines. As early as 1880, the S. D. Warren paper company noted in its annual report that the operation of its Presumpscot mill was often interrupted by the ice that blocked the water intakes in the winter, and by the eels that clogged the millwheels in the fall, bringing the machinery to a complete halt. In the Kennebec watershed, an electrical generating plant on the Sebasticook currently allows no downstream passage for spawning eels, and many big females are killed or more or less crippled passing through the turbines. We do not know what percentage of female eels in the Bay and its tributaries grow to sexual maturity in the Sebasticook, but the historical evidence suggests that it has been an exceptionally important habitat for them throughout most of our history as a piscavorous species in this area. Given the long and variable lapse of time between their arrival in the river and their breeding, and between their breeding and the arrival of the next generation of elvers, we may not know that the eel population is crucially endangered until it is too late to do anything about it.

Meanwhile, Jimmy is out on the water daily from May until September, usually early, when the Bay is quiet and its life is most visible. He sees things, and he sometimes has a surprise waiting for him in his pot—a shad, perch, or immature sturgeon, and, in recent years, more and more catfish, a species that seems to be establishing itself without anyone's much noticing or worrying about it. In the spring, he watches the water and he watches the birds, particularly cormorants. He is not looking for signs of the eels themselves, but for evidence of the Bay's indigenous shiners and white perch, which move up the Cathance to spawn, usually in the second half of May. In his experience, they are a reliable sign that the eels will be emerging from the muddy torpor of their hibernation, and that he should bait and set his pots. In the early part of the season, he finds the fishing best in the smaller rivers: Cathance, Muddy, Abby, and Eastern. Later, they drop down to the deeper and broader waters of the Bay.

It is strange to realize that his eels will wind up in the markets of Hong Kong or Taiwan, still alive and wriggling; as strange as it is to realize that they originated in the Sargasso Sea, or that catching them, in a variety of ingenuous ways, has preoccupied people in our part of the world more or less continuously for six thousand years or so. I don't know any global capitalist who works in a trade of such antiquity, or whose trade would seem to me, as I sit here staring at words on a computer screen a few hundred yards from the Cathance and less than a mile from the Bay, half so desirable.

Smeltville

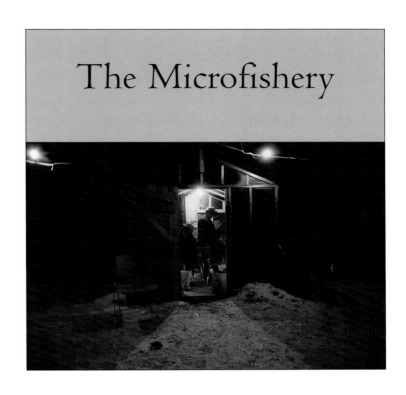

The Microfishery

OCCASIONALLY DURING THE DOLDRUMS OF MIDWINTER, a friend used to take her children smelt fishing. She said there was a small magic in pulling one of the bright little fish into the snug, improvisational domesticity of a smelt shack, warmed by a wood stove, lit by a single lightbulb suspended overhead, and furnished with folding metal chairs or overturned buckets. "And in February," she said, "I'll settle for small magic."

And in February, when the Bay is a jumbled plain of ice, and the river behind our house groans and creaks with the movement of the tides, small magic is worth some investigation.

Smelt belong to the genus *Osmeridae.* They are related to trout and salmon, and somewhat more closely related to the arctic grayling. All of their kinfish are, then, superlative game fish. Smelt would equal or exceed them if they were the size of salmon, or we were the size of squirrels. Their deeply forked tails and streamlined bodies belong to a fish that is built for speed. Their gaping, toothy mouths indicate that they, like bluefish, loan sharks, and high-octane CEOs, are predators. They eat on the run and run on appetite. *Mordax,* the moniker for our particular species, means something like *biting* (cf. *mordant*, as in *mordant wit*). A giant mutant mordant smelt of thirty or forty pounds would look and presumably act a good deal like a barracuda. A big school of them would spread terror and mayhem among swimmers at Reid State Park or Popham Beach, and cause Peter Coviello to migrate to Nebraska. But we are not writing a screenplay here; we are talking about the small magic of the actual creature.

They are anadromous, summering along the coast, seldom more than a mile from shore and seldom in water deeper than twenty feet. In autumn, they move into estuaries and overwinter there, under the ice. They do not like warm water—the preferred temperature range seems to be from the low forties to the mid-fifties. The *Osmerus* genus is circumpolar in its distribution. *O. mordax*—our guy—ranges coastwise from Labrador and Newfoundland as far south as Virginia, but is most abundant from the Saint Lawrence River to Cape Cod. The Bay is thus in the heart of its territory. It is generally known as the rainbow smelt, but is also called frost fish, ice fish, lee fish, and éperlan arc-en-ciel. I have never heard it called anything but smelt in Maine.

AFTER ICE OUT, THEY WRIGGLE UP BROOKS and rills to spawn. These are often small streams that go dry by midsummer. Like salmon, but on a smaller scale, smelt require a swift current, well-oxygenated water, and an unsilted bottom to do

the business of life. The eggs take from eleven to twenty-nine days to hatch, and are somewhat more than one thirty-second of an inch in diameter. At birth, the young are all of a quarter inch long—transparent ribbons equipped with a yolk sac and a pair of dark eyes, which are the most visible things about them. At this stage they have the muscle tone and self-propulsive capacity of damp confetti. Once they reach tidewater, they hang close to the bottom by day, and move up into the shallows to feed at night. When they are about an inch long, they form into schools, and feed largely on zooplankton. As they grow, their tolerance for salinity increases, and they make their way downstream, to richer and cooler waters.

At maturity, the males are smaller than the females, although this is not apparent after their first year, when both average about 5.5 inches in length. They continue to feed on zooplankton, but also small shrimp, mummichogs, and the fry of other fish. By the second year, the males in the only study I have managed to find averaged 7.4 inches, the females 7.8 inches. The fish at this point are sexually mature, and ready to spawn. Some die after a single spawning; many do not. In this, they resemble the Atlantic salmon, not the Pacific ones. By the third year, the males average 8.2 inches and the females 8.6 inches. By the fourth year, each sex has grown another inch, but the rate of increase seems to slow down thereafter.

For all of that, female smelt a foot long are caught from time to time around the Bay, and I have heard of a 14-incher. The International Game Fish Association can tell you to the ounce what the world's record is for every species of trout, grayling, and salmon, caught on any tackle, caught on a three-pound test line, caught by a woman, caught by a minor, and so forth. IGFA lists the world record status of rainbow smelt as VACANT, which would seem to represent a golden opportunity for some ambitious angler. A female minor using a fly rod and a three-pound test line could garner at least four world records for a single fish that wouldn't out-weigh a stick of celery.

On her first spawning, an average female smelt in the study mentioned above carried just over thirty-three thousand eggs; by her third spawning, she carried seventy-six thousand. Because they spawn in such small streams, they do it at night, when gulls and great blue herons are off duty. A female may spawn for as many as four consecutive nights; the males for as many as eight. And so the males substantially outnumber the females on any given night. Dipping smelt from a spawning stream on a cold spring night is a lively sport. In Maine, you are limited to not more than two quarts of smelt per night, if you use this method. There is no limit to how many you can take from an evening of fishing through the ice, and one hears tales of sportsmen staggering out of the camps lugging a five-gallon bucket full of smelt in each hand.

Osmerus MEANS SOMETHING LIKE ODIFEROUS—smelly, in other words. But the odd thing is that the smell is neither unpleasant nor fishy. It is slightly sweet, and closely resembles the smell of a cucumber. The odor disappears if the fish are frozen—it is a sign of freshness. The delicate patina of color on the silver flanks is even more evanescent than its odor. It disappears almost as soon as the fish comes out of the water, but it remains a handsome little creature—the back a pale, watery green, and the sides opalescent and semitransparent, as sleekly shiny as the inside of an onion.

An additional oddity of smelt is that, in winter, they produce a protein that contains glycerol, which is an antifreeze. Only a few species of fish (such as cod, some northern flounders, and herring) do this. Aquaculturists are interested in artificially developing the same capacity in penned salmon, which cannot move to deeper and warmer water in the winter, as their wild siblings do, and so become stressed by the cold, grow slowly, and are susceptible to disease.

Anecdotal evidence, which tends to be corroborated by breathalyzer data randomly collected by state officials, suggest that in the winter smelt fishermen themselves also may undergo significant modification of body chemistry in the course of an evening of sport, which may cause them to stagger out of their camps even if they are not lugging a five-gallon bucket of smelt in each hand.

THE COLONIZATION OF NORTH AMERICA was an unmitigated disaster for almost all native anadromous fish, but for the smelt it was a mitigated disaster. Dams, pollution, siltation, and overfishing all had the usual impacts. For smelt, as for salmon and shad and sturgeon, historical records indicate a staggering abundance. For example, a century and a half ago, dip netters took 750,000 dozen smelt from the Charles River in Watertown, just upstream from Boston. By my arithmetic, that is nine million fish. If they averaged even two ounces apiece, that is over 550 *tons* of smelt. The whole place must have reeked of cucumber. On Prince Edward Island, where they have taken better care of their streams than we have of ours, the commercial harvest still ranges between one and two hundred tons per year. That gives some idea of what we have lost.

But rainbow smelt, like Atlantic salmon, have landlocked populations, particularly in Maine. The landlocked smelt, like the landlocked salmon, are smaller and darker than the seagoing versions, but are genetically indistinguishable from them. And they are, for better or worse, a species that can be "managed." The first experiment in stocking them may have been conducted by Francis Barnard, who was governor of the Massachusetts Bay Colony from 1760–69. He successfully introduced them into Jamaica Pond, just out from Boston. But the real boom in smelt stocking took place in the late nineteenth and early twentieth centuries, fueled by the smelt's reputation as a forage fish upon which game fish could feed and flourish.

The most decisive transplantation came in 1900, when smelt from a lake in Maine were introduced in Crystal Lake in Michigan. It was assumed that this bunch of hapless and unnaturalized immigrants would be eaten for lunch, so to speak, by the big potbellied walleyes in the lake. By the time that the Fish and Game people in Michigan realized that the smelt had turned the tables, and were themselves flourishing on fingerling walleyes, it was too late. The smelt had made their way down into Lake Michigan, where they went to work on the lake trout population, and spread from there into the other Great Lakes and down into the Mississippi-Missouri drainage. They also got into a great many cold-water lakes throughout the upper Midwest and Canada, sometimes smuggled in as illegal aliens, and sometimes brought in as live bait, then dumped heedlessly overboard at the end of the day. So as an invasive landlocked species, they have flourished at the expense of the natives, and benefitted from the same human shortsightedness that has so drastically depleted their coastal populations. There seems to be no effective technique for controlling them, and they have actually become a species of some commercial

Truth in advertising

Open for business

significance in the Great Lakes, Lake Erie in particular.

T HE *MAINE RIVERS* WEBSITE ESTIMATES that in the Kennebec-Androscoggin system, from the ocean to the head of tide on each of the rivers emptying into Merrymeeting Bay, smelt number in the "tens of millions." I do not know how such an estimate is arrived at, but there are undoubtedly a lot of little fish down there under the ice. They come into the rivers late in the fall; one collateral effect of their arrival is that there are always a few seals around the Bay, right up until the time it freezes. I don't know how many smelt it takes to make it worthwhile for a seal to come in from the Atlantic and rub elbows with otters and beavers, but smelt are the only fish that could account for these mighty piscavores being in the Bay so late in the year.

And then when spring finally comes, and the ice breaks, and it is April again, you can go up to Augusta and down to the small waterfront park along the Kennebec. The smelt are moving towards upriver spawning grounds, now accompanied by a flotilla of cormorants. Along the shore men and women stand with big spinning rods. The terminal tackle consists of a two- or three-ounce sinker and, several feet up the line from the sinker, one or two big treble hooks. The anglers cast out as far as possible, let the line sink—how far to let it sink is probably the whole art and science of this kind of fishing—and then sweep the rod back and crank in fast, trying to grapple a smelt. The river is wide and fairly deep here, and the technique looks completely futile—like closing your eyes and trying to grab a four-leaf clover out of your lawn. But the ones who understand what they are doing bring back a smelt or two with virtually every cast. Each angler has a two-quart container—usually a plastic milk bottle cut off at the neck; when it is full, they have their limit. A skilled smelt gaffer can go back to the office after lunch break with enough fish for supper. It's a nice way to bag your own groceries.

In the spring, when there is so much visible life returning, and so much to do, the fact of all these smelt isn't much noticed or appreciated. It is different in the winter. Under the ice, they move in long, shimmering, crowded constellations, as school fish do, seemingly guided by a single impulse. They swirl, spiral, scatter, and coalesce again, veering and flaring in a perfectly synchronized choreography, like silvery filings within a rapidly shifting magnetic field. If you know somebody who actually *pursues* smelt in the winter, moving his camp around—up the rivers in the early part of the season, down toward the Bay by the middle of January, he may take you to a camp that is sitting on mud, close in against the shore. Then the tide rises, there are a few inches of water under the ice, and you start fishing. Nothing happens for a while, and it seems silly—you can look down into the slot of open water where the lines are suspended and see your bait,

Bright lights, little city

Domestic interior. Note full bucket, prominently displayed.

just above the bottom. Then one of the lines twitches, and then another, and soon you are flipping smelt out onto the floor for all you are worth, until you come to your senses and realize that you have all that you need and all that you will be able to persuade your neighbors to take.

More typically, though, you rent one of the camps up the Cathance or Abby, get your bait, trudge out across the ice, and set up shop in your camp. It is a wonderful thing to do with children, because a smelt camp has dollhouse dimensions, and appeals to a child's affinity for miniature facsimiles of the big world. It is also a pretty nice thing to do with a few friends—a precarious snugness there inside the flimsy little shelter, a wood stove you can cook an omelette or heat up a pot of stew on, and plenty of drafty places to keep whatever you are drinking cool, or cold, or frozen solid, according to your preference. Even in talking and laughing, people pay more attention to the lines, suspended from battens along two walls of the shack, than you might expect them to. The water in the races—the slot sawed through the ice on each side of the shack—is very black and the running tide flexes and quickens it, so that the lines quiver slightly. Then—usually at long intervals—the quiver turns into an erratic flutter and somebody snatches the line and pulls *O. mordax* up into the middle of the conversation. It is emphatically and unmistakably No Big Deal. But, sure enough, a small magic.

The camps rent by the tide. When the tide changes, you gather your things together and check out; so does everybody else, and you all walk back toward the shore and the parking lot—the sound of snow crunching under boots, the inky black star-spangled sky, the burning cold of the night air. Everyone is bundled up, hatted and scarfed, toting their coolers and their buckets back toward the imperatives of clock time and ordinary life. The ice is as hard and solid underfoot as the floor of a parking garage, but beneath it is that strange watery world, silent, urgent, and teeming with voracious life. If you have been lucky, it has sent up a few small emissaries to you—food for some small thoughts, and some small fish for the frying pan.

Remnants and Renewals

Eᴀʀʟʏ ɪɴ ᴛʜᴇ Rᴇɢᴀɴ Aᴅᴍɪɴɪsᴛʀᴀᴛɪᴏɴ, I drove to work as usual, by way of the Topsham–Brunswick bridge over the Androscoggin. It was the sort of buttery, coolish May morning to inspire fantasies of truancy, which in my case are never all that far below the surface anyway. And which in my case often must content themselves with a wistful sidewise glance at moving water.

The Androscoggin was low that morning, with only a sluggish current apparent in the big pool at the foot of the dam, upstream from the bridge. Not much food for fantasy there, but even less in the cortege of commuter traffic ahead of me, so I looked down at it. Just a thin apron of water, colored like strong tea or weak coffee, spilling over the lower lip of the pool and into the rapids under the bridge. But then, in the middle of the pool, a heavy swirl, made by something big. What on earth?

When I reached the Brunswick side, I pulled into the parking lot at the old Fort Andros mill, got out, and walked back onto the bridge. The main run of water is on the Brunswick side, then there is an island—a big, bare outcropping of rock—and then the pool on the Topsham side, almost landlocked by the low water. As I approached it, I saw the swirl again, up toward the base of the dam. When I was directly over the pool, I stopped, leaned on the rail, and watched. Nothing, and then more nothing. A couple of joggers came along, paused, jogging in place, to see what I was looking at, saw nothing, and jogged onward, pursuing youth, fitness, vitality; fleeing age, lethargy, terminal inertia. That is what the human race is all about, and it was about time I rejoined it. I would look for a minute more, I told myself, then get back to commuting. I was counting—0 point thirty-seven, 0 point thirty-eight, 0 point thir—when there was the wake of something moving fast, just under the surface. The angle of the light was wrong, I couldn't see what it was—and then it broached: black back, glittering silvery sides—an Atlantic salmon.

I felt happy inside all the rest of that day, as though I'd just privately renegotiated, on much more favorable terms, my lease on life. It was more than just the seeing of a rare creature. The salmon had flipped a switch for me, and the whole Androscoggin drainage, all the way up to the western mountains and Lake Umbagog, had just come on line.

The Clean Rivers Act had been in effect for only a few years, and I was still adjusting to the idea that the Bay and its rivers were fishy places. For several springs, I had seen cormorants busily fishing on the downstream side of the bridge, and striper fishermen had now begun to follow them. I took it as self-evident that the sight of a single salmon implied the presence of others, perhaps of many others. If things continued to improve as dramatically as they had, the day would actually come when I could leave for work a little early, stop off at the Androscoggin, and cast for half an hour or so. I knew what salmon fishing was like—I'd done a little of it over on the Sheepscot and down east on the Machias—and I knew how unlikely one was to take a fly. But I also knew what it looked like to see one roll within casting range, and how the surge of excitement and hope you got from that would easily see you through a month of Mondays.

The day shift at Bath Ironworks concluded at 4:00 P.M.; the commuter traffic would take three-quarters of an hour to subside. At about five o'clock, when I headed home, I was able to drive very slowly back across the bridge, watching the pool. Nothing. I stopped on the Topsham side, got out, and watched from there. More nothing. Supper beckoned. I looked at that pool every time I crossed the bridge that year, and I still do now, even at times of the year when no fish could possibly be in it. I never saw another salmon there. Each year, a few have come up the fish ladder at the dam—some years more, some years less, never many.

T HE FIRST COMMERCIAL HARVESTING OF SALMON on the Androscoggin occurred in 1673, at the foot of Pejepscot Falls, four miles upriver from the head of tide. It amounted to ninety kegs of salmon, with shortage of salt, not of salmon, being the limiting factor. The French and Indian Wars delayed full commercial exploitation of the Androscoggin salmon, but by 1788 peace between the colonial powers was well established in these parts, and the one-sided war of Euro-Americans against anadromous fish was in full swing. That year, we find citizens from Brunswick petitioning the State of Massachusetts to put an end to excessive seining, weir fishing, and dip netting: "...if not speedily stopped, [these practices] will end in the final ruin of fish in Merrymeeting Bay and the rivers running into the same." Fifty years later, citizens along the Androscoggin were petitioning again, this time against the construction of illegal dams, up and down the river. The new legislature up in Augusta responded in the same way that the old one down in Boston had—it speedily did nothing. Salmon were money; but water power was more money. And the right of people to make money and more money without interference or supervision by the government, and without consideration for their neighbors or neighborhoods, was turning out to be an unstated, fundamental premise of the American Revolution.

Within its first fifteen miles above Brunswick, the Androscoggin had four waterfalls: at Pejepscot, at Lisbon Falls, at Lewiston, and at Brunswick itself, where the river pitched sharply down to tidewater. Within the first fifteen miles above the head of tide in Augusta, the Kennebec had only a few small rapids. So the Androscoggin offered both better places for catching salmon, as they congregated below the falls and fought their way up over them, and for building dams and putting the river to work. Salmon migration consequently died more quickly and completely there than on the Kennebec, where even now the process is not absolutely, indisputably complete. For as long as I have lived in Maine, there have been reports of salmon from Bond Brook in Augusta and Togus Stream in Randolph, both tributaries of the tidal reaches of the Kennebec. Sometimes the reports involved poachers with grappling hooks, and sometimes they came from fisheries experts. These could be poignant: back in the 1960s, one of the experts, Matthew Scott, watched juvenile salmon parr congregate on one side of Togus Stream, to avoid the plume of raw sewage being discharged from the Togus Veterans Administration Hospital. Whether these fish and those spawned in Bond Brook were a remnant of the original, indigenous Kennebec salmon, or whether they represented strays from the stocking of Atlantic salmon in the Penobscot has been a hot topic of debate, a sort of piscatorial conflation of the right-to-life and the death-with-dignity questions. Where does hope begin, and when must we conclude, reluctantly or otherwise, that it has ended?

The history of this debate on the Kennebec began in the 1830s with the first damming of the river. By the middle of the decade, there were four dams between Ticonic Falls in

Waterville, the first natural barrier to upstream navigation on the river, and Great Falls in Skowhegan, sixteen miles further upstream. Two of these dams completely obstructed the river. During that period—1830–37, to be precise—a drift netter named Charles Hume plied his trade below the falls in Waterville. He averaged 150 salmon per season and estimated the annual catch in that section of the river to be 2,000. In 1837 construction of what came to be called the Edwards Dam began in Augusta. By the following year it was complete, so Hume moved his operation downriver and had himself a banner year, landing between 300 and 400 of the suddenly dispossessed and disoriented salmon that milled around below the dam. But that was just about the end of it. He kept at it—it is the nature of fishermen to keep at it— but by 1850 he was catching no more than four or five salmon a year, and in some years none at all.

Faith, or force of habit, or the refusal of memory to accept loss as ever being final and irrevocable must have been what brought him back to the river each spring, to play his nets out across the current and drift down with them, watching the floats and hoping to see one suddenly twitch, bob, and skid off across the surface. Apparently, something of the same stubborness or wishful thinking afflicted the salmon: the few that Mr. Hume would catch; the few—a hundred a year, three or four hundred a year—that would be caught more or less accidentally by drift netters and weir fishermen

for at least fifty years after the construction of the dam; and the few that continue to be reported every year—adults seen jumping below the dam in Augusta, juvenile fish in Bond Brook and Togus Stream. And now at last, after protracted negotiation, the Edwards Dam has come down. Striped bass, shad, and sturgeon can again run as far upriver as Waterville for the first time in a century and a half. Salmon redds— nests—have been documented in the main stream of the Kennebec itself, in the gravelly shallows between Waterville and Augusta.

We don't, of course, know how it will all work out. Since anadromous fish last used this section of the river, newcomers have moved in: smallmouth bass and brown trout, both introduced as sports fish and both thriving. The dam removal that restores upstream access for sea-run fish also opens it to carp, a Eurasian transplant whose bottom-feeding habits may not bode well for salmon eggs, any more than the smallmouth bass and trout bode well for the salmon fry, or the stripers bode well for those species and their fry.

But at least for the present, the watershed of possibility has been expanded. The glass is no longer 99.9 percent empty, insofar as the Kennebec salmon are concerned. It is now perhaps 00.1, or even 00.2 percent full. That is not reason to relax and celebrate. The patient is still in intensive care, and will be for a long time to come.

But one of the oldest cultural myths we have is the myth

Alewives

of the Saving Remnant. The Old and New Testaments are full of it, as is subsequent Judaeo-Christian theology; the story of Aeneas and his wretched little band of refugees from Troy is a secular version of it; the Puritan settlers of New England were sustained through privations and hard winters by the conviction that they themselves embodied it. What the Saving Remnant saves is never simply itself and its own posterity. It promises something fuller and wider: the restoration of a sacred benediction that had been abused, ignored, or taken for granted, and so replaced by a curse, a blight upon the land. The Kennebec–Androscoggin history since the arrival of the Europeans can be telescoped into a single image—the raw, untreated discharge from the veterans' hospital at Togus, billowing from the outlet pipe like smoke out of a smokestack, fanning outward as it descends the stream. And a part of that image, crowded against the opposite bank, are those salmon parr that Matthew Scott saw, back in the 1960s: a pathetic remnant, the very last or the very first syllables of an ancient story.

THE STORY OF COMMERCIAL FISHING IN THE BAY, the rivers that flow into it, and the river that flows out of it is the story of anadromous fish. To get it, you basically talk to old-timers until you find that you have become one yourself, passing on an uncertain amalgam of observation and hearsay. As far as I know, the first really systematic attempt to tell that story came in the form of the *Twelfth Annual Report of the Maine Board of Agriculture*, published in Augusta in 1867. Its authors, Nathan W. Foster and Charles G. Atkins, were not concerned with conservation as an end in itself. They spoke for one of the competing interests—commercial fishing—within a rural and regional economy that still had the production of food as the source of much of its wealth and many of its worries.

Among the old-timers they talked to was Mr. Hume, the salmon netter whose business was first relocated and eventually liquidated by the Edwards Dam. They also ascended rivers all over the state, studied dams and spawning grounds, gathered all the fishy data they could find, and tried to estimate the past, present, and future values of particular fisheries in particular watersheds. They had relatively little to say about the Androscoggin beyond noting that it had been more than fifty years since salmon were last seen even as far upriver as Lewiston, and that alewives, which formerly bred in ponds that drained into the river, had disappeared entirely. The culprits were the dams at Brunswick, Pejepscot, Lisbon Falls, and Lewiston. They judged that fishways could feasibly be installed on the three lower dams, with great potential benefit: "It is a noble river, and so far as we have examined, promises an easy task and great results to the cultivation [i.e., stocking] of salmon."

Their examination of the Kennebec and its many greater

and lesser tributaries is far more detailed, and includes in it Merrymeeting Bay, the Cathance, Abagadasset, and Eastern Rivers, as well as the tidal portion of the Androscoggin. They describe the fish weirs deployed around the Bay and in the river below the Chops: their design, cost, and productivity, the months they were in use, and the species they targeted. They interviewed drift-netters and seiners, and refer to bag nets set beneath the ice for taking smelt.

They make it clear that the tidewater fishery was the only significant one left on the Kennebec, and that it was greatly diminished from what it had been. "The statement is very generally made, and it appears to be fact, that the most of the shoal water weirs [the type used in the Kennebec downstream from the Chops] do not pay." They cost $50 or $60 dollars to build, and had to be rebuilt every spring. On average, they might produce $300 worth of fish, from which the cost of labor, salt, packaging, and shipping had to be deducted. Deepwater weirs, used chiefly in the Bay and its tributaries, cost $300–400 to build and the gross value of their catch ran from $600–800 per season, an even lower rate of return.

In 1866 there had been forty deepwater weirs around the Bay, and twenty shallow-water weirs in the river below it. Those in the Bay were by far the more productive, harvesting 160,000 shad, compared to 40,000 downriver, and 1,000,000 alewives, compared to 150,000 downriver. In all

weirs that year, the incidental by-catch of salmon was guesstimated at no more than a hundred, but the next year, while less productive of shad and alewives, saw 1,200 salmon taken, the majority of them downriver from the Bay.

Foster and Atkins made no effort to estimate the size of the smelt harvest, although they noted that the catch was substantial, especially in the weirs that were constructed specifically for them in the fall. They make no mention of eels or sturgeon. In the case of eels, this may have been prejudice; in the case of sturgeon, it was because no market existed. That would change radically in another twenty years or so, when caviar established itself as a high prestige food among the wealthiest European and American gourmands, and brought on two or three decades of remorseless overfishing in the Kennebec and every other sturgeon river on either coast of America.

Foster and Atkins were most concerned by the decline of the shad fishery. Thirty years before, there were only two weirs on the Bay (although apparently many more in the lower river). Even so, drift netters on the Cathance and Eastern Rivers alone caught and barreled more shad for export than had been collected from all forty of the Bay's weirs in 1867. They also note the virtual disappearance of mature striped bass from the Bay, although young ones—four inches or less in length—continued to show up in the bag nets of smelt fishermen from time to time. An informant told them of having seen, some unspecified number of years earlier, big striped bass caught through the ice on the Eastern River "in such numbers as to sink the ice on which they were deposited." Does this mean, among other things, that this voracious predator once found enough forage fish—smelt? shad fry? eels?—to overwinter in the Bay in great numbers?

Foster and Atkins attributed the decline of Maine's fisheries to impassable dams, overfishing, and pollution. Fishways could be built, and regulations as to when, where, how, and how many fish might be caught could be enacted and enforced. Pollution, they felt, was less demonstrable in its effects, and they concluded, probably in good faith, that it required further study.

Their admirable report was useless. Tidewater fisheries belonged to a disappearing economy; the industrial economy that was replacing it had interests that were at every point antithetical to those of fish and fishermen. By the time I got to Maine, just over a century after the publication of the report, the industrial economy was itself becoming a thing of the past, but it appeared that the damage had been done, terminally. My first few years of commuting over the Androscoggin were grim—on most mornings, you'd rather look at the traffic than the river. A frothy, iridescent foam, with here and there a patch of water visible through it, was what you saw. After the spring floods, twigs hanging out over the water were draped with a filmy stuff, and if you went smelt fishing in the winter, your line came up out of the water coated with a mucilaginous slime. In summer the algae blooms made the water so murky you could not see a foot deep into it, and in warm weather there were regular fish kills—mostly suckers and runty little perch, because that was mostly what lived there at that season. The Kennebec and the Androscoggin appeared to have been written off as rivers—they were sluices and sewers. Because I was a newcomer, having no sense of what these rivers had been and therefore of what they might be, I fatalistically wrote them off myself, at least that part of them between their headwaters, where trout swam, and the Bay, where, as I had quickly found out, ducks and geese showed up in big numbers, every spring and every fall.

T WO WEEKS AGO WAS THE FIRST WEEK of the 2005 duck season. We had had a cool, wet spring and early summer, a hot, dry August, and a mild September, with a lot of rain. I was out by myself, off the Abagadasset mouth. There is a long, sandy-bottomed marsh between the mouth of the river and the Kennebec, and the rice in it, this year as most years, was very good. The marsh has several channels cutting through it, from the Abby side to the Kennebec side; the tide was rising and pushing strongly through those channels. The day was definitive, classic, the day I see in my mind's eye when I think of the Bay: windless, with a thin, milky wash of cloud to filter and soften the blues and blue-grays of sky and water.

I had taken the motor off the transom and was sculling the gunning float along the southern end of the marsh. Once I got to the Kennebec, I would have the tide with me, and could slip along the outer edge of the marsh without much effort, and maybe jump a mallard or black duck there. But sculling against the current to get there was stiff work. I was in water not more than two feet deep, over a hard-packed sand bottom scalloped and corrugated by the current; the tide was coming urgently now, bending the bullrushes at the edge of the current, visibly pulsing through the little channel. There was a fast, emphatic splash in the water beside me—a fish, and it was not a carp. Then a flurry of slashing strikes—I was in the middle of a school of small stripers feeding on bait fish. In the shallow water I could see the stripers pretty clearly—the fast pale shapes under the surface, the flank or tail of one thrashing for a moment in the air, close enough, if I had been quick enough, for me to reach out and touch. They were small, not much over a foot long. In general, they seemed to be pinning the bait against the bottom—I could see an occasional dim flicker when the school veered and their silvery sides caught the light.

It didn't last long. The tide swept the bait on through the channel, and the stripers followed. When I reached the Kennebec, looking straight across toward the Chops, I could see a small cloud of gulls and terns, hovering and dipping over the water. Their cries came to me very faintly. The surface of the Bay was glassy, but directly beneath the birds was a quarter of an acre of erupting water. At the distance I was, it was hard to make out individual splashes, but it seemed to me that the commotion there suggested bigger fish. Normally, when I have seen stripers doing this, the flurry moves across the water like a squall, then suddenly disappears. But something about the currents swirling in through the Chops must have kept the school of bait fish more or less stationary, or was continually funneling more of them into the same place. As I coasted almost effortlessly along the edge of the marsh, I kept looking back toward the Chops. The blitz out in the middle of the Bay lasted for forty-five minutes, moving slightly to the south as the tide rose.

Later, I surprised myself with a nifty passing shot on a hen mallard. And later still, the wind came up strongly, and when I looked southward into the Androscoggin mouth, I could see a fog coming my way, slowly erasing the landscape behind it. By quitting time, I was fogbound myself, with the wind still rising and the Bay suddenly a very different place—not pastoral any more but chill and oceanic. I hugged the dim loom of the shore; even so, I went astray a couple of times before I got safely back into the Cathance, where even I could not possibly get off course again. It was completely dark, and I was pretty wet and chilled, by the time I reached

An ocean of fog

our dock, secured the boat, and walked up the path toward the house, its lights a soft blur through the foggy woods, like something from a fairy tale.

I knew that, falling asleep that night, I would replay the afternoon to myself. The duck had confirmed the day. But the deeper happiness of it had been finding myself surrounded by small stripers, and then seeing that big school feeding far out, the gulls and terns fluttering and crying over it. I did not at the time think about the way the rivers and the Bay had been thirty years ago. On another day—today, to be specific—I could editorialize and moralize about it, put it in the context of a continuing history. But the quality of the happiness, in seeing the scene and then in remembering it, had nothing to do with thinking, in any ordinary sense of the word. It was simply a matter of having been where I had been and seen what I had seen, more or less in my own backyard.

Biologists from Maine's Department of Marine Resources seine for anadromous fry

Newcomers

EVEN BEFORE THE CLEAN RIVERS ACT went into effect, carp were abundant in the Bay, and they still are. In May, when the wild rice and bullrushes are just a stubble on the mudflats, they become active, feeding up into guzzles as the tide rises, fanning out as it covers the flats. Flushed in shallow water, they rush off like torpedoes, leaving vapor trails of dissolving mud. Later in the summer, when the marsh is thick and high and the tide is half up, you can watch reeds stirring and waving, or the sudden, mysterious agitation of a patch of pickerel weed, as though a very local breeze had set it astir, and follow one's progress as it rummages across what must be a carp's dream of the Elysian Fields, hog heaven for a fish that is, in its thickset, slope-shouldered body, its way of rooting for food, and its love of muck, distinctly swinish.

And, like pigs, carp have had a longstanding intimacy with human beings, one which began in Asia where the fish are still raised commercially, often in rice paddies, and which exists in this country in the form of the goldfish that were developed from them—a genetic equivalent of developing silk purses from sows' ears. From Asia carp spread progressively westward; by the fourteenth century, they had reached

England. They were widely established there by the time that Sir Izaak Walton wrote *The Compleat Angler* in 1653. He surmised that their propagation had been facilitated by their extraordinary toughness—they could be kept alive for a considerable time in a coarse cloth sack full of damp moss. He deemed them, as few in Bowdoinham would, "the queen of rivers; a stately, a good, and a very subtle fish."

They made it to North America in the 1870s, under the sponsorship of our federal government. The thought was that they would provide an important food source, to replace native species that had been reduced by overfishing, habitat degradation, and pollution. From our vantage point, this looks like a last effort to shore up a myth or a memory of our continent as a place of such inexhaustible abundance that its citizens could to a substantial degree feed themselves as the original hunter-gatherers had, by harvesting the uncultivated bounty of nature. The carp themselves, at least, found a reality to match the myth, and now flourish in every state of the Lower Forty-eight, which suggests their remarkable adaptability. They came into the Bay without official sponsorship; somebody caught one in a drift net, to the best of local memory, in 1948 or so, had no idea what it was, and hoped it might be rare or valuable. A year or two later, Ronnie Burrell had a bait weir—for catching alewives to sell to lobstermen—up the Abby, and caught quite a few. Now their numbers are legion, and if you fly over the Bay at low water,

you can look down and see them along the edges of the channels, waiting like Christmas shoppers for the rising tide to open the mudflats for business.

It is hard to believe that any of their habitats suit them better than Merrymeeting Bay. If you knew nothing of the fish's history and distribution, you might easily conclude that it had evolved with specific reference to this particular place, and was tailor-made to feed on the vegetation and micro-organisms of the mudflats: big enough not to worry about osprey, heron, or mink when it ventured into the shallows; powerful enough to have no difficulty with currents; and, judging from its abundance, able to browse and mooch widely and contentedly down toward the lower end of the food chain, where more specialized and fastidious fish offered no competition.

Their happiness has been further abetted by *Homo euroamericanus*, who not only brought them to this Eden of rivers, estuaries, and fertile mud, but have also thus far disdained to do what people had done quite cheerfully in Eurasia—harvest and eat them. There may come a day when people here will look back with a kind of incredulity at the swarming and despised carp of Merrymeeting Bay—the same incredulity with which we read those benevolently intended colonial ordinances that prohibited local farmers from feeding their laborers salmon every day of the week.

On a rainy Saturday afternoon in May, I drove across the Cathance River bridge in Bowdoinham. The eye always turns toward water. The tide was falling, and the brown river, swollen by the spring rains, ran strongly in mid-stream, spawning a slow, purposeful eddy in the deep water against the east bank. On the bank itself I saw, for the first time this spring, a group of generically familiar but individually unrecognizable people who, without anyone's knowing their names, have become part of our local meteorology, harbingers of summer. They were fishing for whatever might bite, emphatically including carp. On an impulse, I decided to speak to them, and pulled over into the gravel lot where Jimmy McPherson parks his smelt camps in the off-season.

The first of these people had been the Kims, who were, with the help of the Bowdoinham Baptist Church, settled in the town as refugees from Cambodia. The church did all it could to ease their coming: got their children started in the Bowdoinham elementary school, where they were classmates and objects of endless fascination to our middle daughter, a second-grader at the time; found employment for Mr. Kim; helped him and his family maintain connections with other citizens of what had been their country, their world, and who had, like them, ended up in our country, our world, in places like Bowdoinham, Lewiston, Hallowell, and Gray. I'm certain that the Baptists also offered up many prayers for

them, in addition to all the practical assistance.

But I am also sure that gods, like locations or languages, cannot enter people so radically and violently displaced as the Kims were, and magically give them consolation, wisdom, or a sense of what life means and offers in an utterly unintelligible place. God, or gods, enter us through mundane intermediaries—culture, education, gossip, work, holidays, childhood games, people all around us in whom we can recognize godliness or ungodliness. As our daughter reported on her exotic classmates, who spoke no English and excited all of her own Christian and maternal instincts, I tried to imagine what it was like for the Kims trying to reconstruct life here, where even the seasons must have seemed like something from a different planet. What did they feel when the chill, ominously lengthening shadows fell across the world in the fall, and when the river became skimmed over with grayish ice that looked at first like the scum that forms on a cooling pot of soup, and then turned into something solid and earthlike, with Jimmy's village of smelt shacks lined up in a tidy row where there had been water?

The family had been installed in a small, dark cinderblock house near the Community School, so that Hing and Teng, the two little girls, could walk there with their father every day. There was also an infant in the family, born in a Thai refugee camp. A fourth child had died during the terrible journey out of Cambodia and into Thailand, whether by disease, starvation, or more direct agency of the Khmer Rouge we did not know. Mr. Kim worked as a janitor at the school. I would see him there—a small man, trim and compact in his custodial uniform. There was something you could mistake for vindictiveness in the steady, intense way he worked, and he projected an isolation from the people passing up and down the halls that could not have been greater if he had been born deaf, blind, and mute.

The Kims stayed in Bowdoinham for perhaps five years, then moved, and the last we heard they were living in Florida. We hear that Hing has married—her church sponsors, our neighbors, went down for the wedding, and were pleased and happy about the ceremony, the groom, and how things seemed to be going for the whole family. So it seems that the process is continuing which will one day allow Hing or her children or grandchildren to look at some particular American neighborhood and simply think *home*, without any emotions beyond the ordinary ones that are in the word itself.

But before the Kims moved away from Bowdoinham, Mr. Kim noticed the river. I like to imagine that it was after his first winter here, when the ice was at last gone, the rushes were emerging, the willows had turned that delicate green of early leaf, and we had had a day or so of steamy warmth. After all the numbing things that had happened, his own country must have come to seem a private Eden-myth for him—less a place he had actually lived in than a kind of

hypothesis to account for the desolation and remoteness of the place he lived in now. That place he wouldn't see again had been warm, luxuriant, and river-laced, its life sustained by the ingenious hydrology of rice paddies, the careful creation, over many generations, of a landscape of small, enclosed freshwater marshes, governed by artificial tides. Gathering fish, in one fashion or another, would have been a familiar thing, almost like the harvesting of another crop. And so perhaps the Cathance, as it took on its summer lushness, came to him like a whisper of his own language, reassuring him by its sudden familiarity, and suggesting the possibility of fish.

In any event, the Kims, often accompanied by another family or two, began fishing in the Cathance that spring. They must have had some luck, and they certainly had no competition. The word apparently spread in Maine's Cambodian community. Now, with the Kims having relocated to Florida, the tradition they started here still flourishes, every spring and summer. In glum, wet weather there may be only three or four men standing by the river, hunched and dripping. But more typically, there are whole families.

At first, these strangers confined themselves to the road shoulders immediately along the bridge abutments. I think they were doing what people must always do when in a new place and unsure of their rights and local customs: they were squatting, incrementally establishing a territory. They at first avoided Bowdoinham's public landing, with its picnic tables and dock, because others congregated there, but now they fish there too, and range further downstream from there, toward the Bay. At low tide, the boys and younger men may slog out along the mudflats for a quarter mile or so and station themselves. Sometimes they rest one foot on top of the other, or curl it behind the calf of the opposite leg, so that they are temporarily one-legged, and resemble herons. And, if you go by in a boat, they watch you covertly, as a heron would, ready to take flight, but not to concede their right to be there. If you wave, they wave back, expressionlessly.

Back up behind them, these more adventurous men leave wives, mothers, and small children. Some of these also fish, but on the whole they suggest a band of gypsies, professional travelers momentarily encamped in Bowdoinham. There are a few aluminum-framed folding chairs, perhaps a ragged blanket or two for the smallest children to play on, food, bait buckets, the general impression of a low-budget yard sale. It all looks pastoral, local, and comfortable. You could not guess the history behind it if you did not happen to know it, and knowing it, you still cannot imagine it or how it came to eventuate in this sweet scene.

So, crossing the Cathance River bridge that particular Saturday afternoon in May, I stopped. With the drizzle the weather felt raw, as though we'd moved back into mud season. A woman was there in Jimmy's parking lot, fixing food

Spring, incoming tide. Wild rice, just emerging, is pale green; bulrushes are darker and taller.

by a beat-up van. Two children stood attentively by; two others, slightly older, played among the off-duty smelt shacks. Four men were across the road; one, a boy really, was walking back toward the van, perhaps for food. I smiled at him and he smiled, but anxiously, diffidently. I asked him if the fishing was good. "Good," he agreed. "Good, good."

I crossed the road to where the others were fishing. They had of course seen me stop, but they kept their eyes focused on the water as I approached them. I spoke to the nearest one, asking him if they were having much luck. He appeared to be older than I am, which is not young, but he nodded eagerly, like a child who had expected a rebuke and did not get it. Just then his rod twitched and he cranked in fast—an old open-faced spinning reel that grated and rattled like a coffee grinder. It was a yellow perch, not as big as a drumstick. He unhooked it and tossed it in a plastic bucket. There were five or six identically sized perch already in the bucket, and a hornpout that was slightly larger. And underneath them all, a carp. It was indeed a stately fish, bronze, with a clear, serene eye. Its gills were flexing unhurriedly, as though it were taking deep breaths, calming and bracing itself. It must have weighed five or six pounds, and looked huge in the bucket with the perch—Gulliver among the Lilliputians. I whistled and asked the man if he had caught him. He shook his head no, and pointed to one of the others, who allowed himself to look shyly pleased.

But it was clear that I was making them nervous, and would for as long as I stayed. It was their place. I asked the man if they often caught carp that big here. He said he didn't know; he hadn't fished here before. He said they were from Connecticut; friends had told them about this place, that it was a good place, a good place to fish. I said it looked like the friend was right, and he said "Yes, yes. A good place. Good fun, you know." I wished him luck and he thanked me, his eyes never leaving the point where the line entered the water.

As I walked back to my truck, the two older children, one in hot pursuit of the other, dashed out from among the smelt shacks, nearly colliding with me. They looked up and giggled, covering their mouths with their hands. Their eyes were bright with the excitement of whatever game they'd been playing. They darted back between two shacks. For this present moment, they were simply two very happy children, on a chill, fresh-smelling May afternoon in Bowdoinham, with the rain, which had slackened briefly, now beginning to start back up, the drops dimpling in the eddy and in the sleek, remorseless current beyond it.

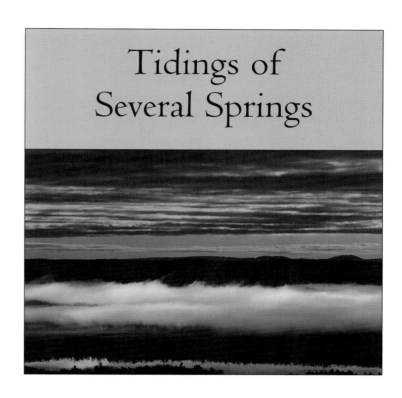

Tidings of
Several Springs

CLOCKS AND CALENDARS MARK TIME into uniform, modular units. An hour is never less than sixty minutes, a week never more than seven days. It gets a little dicier when we come to months and years—how many days hath October? Leap year? But by and large our subdivisions of time are stable, and thus readily convertible into the equally uniform, regular units of dollars and cents. Our jobs, our careers, our conception of life is based on the notion that time essentially is, whether we like it or not, money.

It is something of a revelation to be reminded, even momentarily, that time is an unmetered flow, not something that we do or don't have to spare. The revelation is likeliest to come in the spring.

In summer and winter there's a sense of sameness and stasis—both seasons can feel permanent, as though they have been granted tenure. The trees are in leaf, or they are bare; the migratory species are in residence or *in absentia;* children are on vacation or they are in school. From day to day, business is as usual. In fall, the withdrawal of light and life is quiet; things fade away. Birds gather into flocks but do not sing; amphibians, long since silent and mostly invisible anyway, are not missed when they bury themselves and go to sleep for four or five months. Insects thin out and vanish, and we hardly notice.

But, beginning in March and reaching a crescendo in May, spring is a series of awakenings, arrivals, and revivals. Everything seems to be in movement. The ice breaks up on the Bay, and big floes slosh back and forth on the tides; the solid earth turns first to mud and then to grass, which comes up through the dead thatch of last year's lawns and pastures, grows faster than an average American male, in good health and reasonably fit, can push a lawn mower, and ripples and skitters like water when the winds gust over it, tossing and tormenting the dandelions on their stalks. The woods are as quiet and calm and sparse as the inside of a Quaker meeting house, and then the leaves unfurl, the vegetation closes in, insects buzz and bite, and warblers flit through the canopy, eluding the binoculars.

New England's spring weather is famously variable. Mark Twain claimed to have counted one hundred and thirty-six different kinds of it in a twenty-four-hour period, and that was in Connecticut. He was bragging and complaining, as we all do. The Bay can be sleek, a soft dove-gray mirror of an overcast, mild morning sky, and an invitation to truancy. By the time you've put the canoe on the truck, rounded up your paddles and another paddler, and gotten down to the landing, the wind has come up and the Bay looks like a bad day

somewhere off the coast of Newfoundland.

Everything is process and urgency; schedules clash; the air controllers are on strike and the pilots are on Ecstasy. One morning the yard is full of big, fluffed out robins, prospecting for worms; blackbirds and grackles wheeze and grate and clatter in the fields, and the thin cry of a killdeer comes down from overhead. Late in March, fox sparrows show up—yesterday there were none; today there are half a dozen. They scratch among the dead leaves with both feet at once, which makes them look as though they were standing in place and skipping rope. They are the most handsome of the sparrows and won't stay long, but while they are here they repossess our yard as officiously and confidently as the hens have repossessed the hen yard, now that the snow is out of it. And have at last, after a long siege of layer's block, resumed production—an egg a hen a day, a fine clutch of them waiting for you every morning in the suddenly warm, close, ammonia-reek of the henhouse.

You want to be up and doing, getting ahead of the season that is coming at you like a tsunami. But the weather prevents you, or the mud. You can't yet mow, can't yet plant. You can go for a walk out on Center Point, hear the wind in the big pines and oaks that grow on the ridge of glacial till at the end of the point, and, if you are lucky, see a pair of eagles playing in the wind, just over the tree tops. The game they play is you-be-the-osprey-and-I'll-be-the-eagle, immedi-

Ice out, late March

ately followed by I'll-be-the-osprey-and-you-be-the-eagle. It's courtship, or pair-bonding—prenuptial whoopee that even the immature ones engage in. At the edge of a pasture at dusk, you can catch a woodcock doing the same thing, lightly turning its fancy to thoughts of love: first expressing the tender passion by means of a plaintive, subdued little noise, as though it were, in the most tactful and unassertive way possible, farting, and then launching up into its astonishing, twittering, spiraling flight.

The chancy weather of April—ahead of itself, behind itself—produces some strange sights—a woodcock huddled in the middle of a snowy pasture, its cryptic plumage making it shockingly obvious; a marbled salamander exploring the little freshet that runs through our cellar, moving with the ponderous, cautious deliberation of an astronaut walking on the moon. One bright morning, hearing a scrabbling above the damper in our chimney, I opened the damper and a kestrel, of all things, dropped down onto the hearth, flew to a window, fluttered against it, and tangled himself in the curtains. It was a beautiful little male, his plumage as vivid as a songbird's. I got my hands around him, took him out the front door, threw him up like a bride tossing a bouquet, and watched him rejoin the wild, buffeting winds of an April morning. Go fly a kite? Pooh. Go fly a kestrel, if you want to see something that lives in the wind.

Once we had high, high winds and heavy, heavy rains.

The Bay was flooded and tempestuous, and every duck on it took refuge in a temporary half-acre puddle in the strawberry fields of east Bowdoinham. The water was carpeted with them; others stood or waddled gravely around on the furrowed ground; and still others continued to arrive, boring through a rain that came almost horizontal. The wind in the hedgerow trees bordering the field sounded like surf beating against rocks. You could see the ducks, mostly blacks and mallards, quacking—they looked like ventriloquists' dummies without the ventriloquists, because you could hear nothing. Then the wind would relent for a moment and you could suddenly hear them, loud and raucous. A few pintails were mixed into the flock, the drakes in their breeding plumage as trim, spruce, and imperturbable as gentlemen in tuxedos, crowded in together with ordinary folk on a rush-hour subway platform. When we got out of the car to see better, every duck raised its head and watched us, and the ones nearest us began edging away, but none offered to fly.

The Great April Blizzard of 1982 gave us two feet of snow—not wet, ephemeral, springtime stuff, but the genuine powdery, drifting, blowing, midwinter article—and it refroze the waters. I had made up my mind, weather or no weather, to clean out the chicken house the next day, and so I did, shoveling a winter's worth of litter into an oversized cardboard box and hauling it on a toboggan to the edge of the garden, where I emptied it out in a heap and left it there to age itself into hen dressing, rich manure for our chronically undernourished asparagus.

The next morning I looked out the window, and there was my manure pile, the only thing unsnowed under and unfrozen over in the entire landscape. And there, picking around in it, ferreting out bits of spilled or undigested grain, was a drake wood duck. He stayed for a week, withdrawing into a clump of lilacs when he was not feeding but never abandoning this one tiny island of nutrition in our neo-glacial landscape. A drake wood duck is a creature of extravagant, opulent beauty, being to the lilies of the field as the lilies of the field were to Solomon arrayed in all his glory. And neither the lilies nor Solomon at his finest could have looked more out of place than the little drake. The light reflecting up from the snow illuminated him as though he were in a photographer's studio, posing for a formal portrait, and he did not look real. When withdrawn into the lilacs, he tucked his head down snug against his breast and looked to be asleep, but if we stepped outside, the head came up instantly, and he watched our every movement, craning his neck and shifting uneasily. I think he must from time to time have flown somewhere—perhaps down to the Cathance bridge, where the river never freezes—to drink, but his absences were brief, and he stayed with us until rain and warm weather took the snow, and April got back to being April.

THINGS THAT EXIST HAVE A PARALLEL EXISTENCE as images in our minds. That is what makes them real for us. We have a platonic idea of the other seasons in New England, and know what we mean when we speak of typical summer, or autumn, or winter weather. We mean, respectively, a high blue sky, reflected in glittering blue water along the rockbound coast, or a high blue sky with a row of flaming maples thrusting up into it; or a high blue sky over a glittering, undulant expanse of snow, diamond-bright beneath it. These are not the only kinds of summer, autumn, and winter weather, but when they occur they have a perfection that suggests that they are the true epitome and essence of the season. We measure any particular day of any given season, and any particular season of any given year against this standard and grade it accordingly. A run of snowless, rainy, or mild winters can set us to grumbling in the elderly, moralistic, don't-make-'em-like-they-usetah fashion that is one of the symptoms and consolations of growing old.

In thirty-six years, and counting, of living in Maine, I've never heard anybody speak of a typical Maine spring, or describe what it should look like, or what a perfect spring day would be. Springtime grumbling is like the grumbling of a political party out of power—an implacable dissatisfaction with the terrible mess that things are in, but no real conception of an alternative to it. One senior colleague of mine told me that everything fell apart in the spring; that more old people gave up and died then than in any other season; that the rates of divorce and intramural homicide peaked in March. And that less predictable manifestations of psychic and spiritual distress were also likeliest to occur then, as, for example, that very year when a motorist drove slowly down Maine Street in Brunswick in the small hours, turned up onto the sidewalk, and bashed his car through the plate-glass windows of several storefronts before abandoning it inside a department store, in the men's wear section. He told the police that he was protesting the town's snow removal policy, but the consensus of humane opinion was that he was protesting March, and everyone felt a secret sympathy and admiration for him for doing it.

Another colleague countered that we did, however, get some lovely May weather; the only trouble was, we got it in June.

What is typical, or at least comparable and measurable from one year to the next, are the arrivals, emergences, and revivals: a woodcock once heard on the ninth of March, the earliest date ever; the first geese clamoring, a noise that comes down faintly from very high up, and takes a moment to recognize after so long an absence; the first wood frogs, cluttering in the boggy corner of a pasture, then, a day or two later, the first peepers, shrilling through a sleet storm.

Robert Frost's hill wife, surrounded by emptiness and fearing that it is growing inside her, felt that there was something wrong with having to feel so glad when the birds returned in the spring, singing "whatever it is they sing." His New England still had that kind of loneliness in it: physical isolation, abandoned farms, habits of silence, withdrawal, dawn-to-dark-labor. Our New England doesn't, unless you count Swan Island, where the memory of it has been frozen in time. We bear a lot more resemblance to commuters around Boston or Atlanta than to the hill wife and the other inhabitants of Frost's poems. Our world is ruled less by weather and geography than by clock time and calendar time, salaries, interest rates, leading economic indicators, the evening news on television. The local reality, the local news, the local weather have a diminished significance.

For us now, the birds that return, the frogs that awaken, the shiners that dimple the surface of the Cathance, telling Jim McPherson that it is time to set his eel pots, serve to remind us that *time* and *tide* were once synonymous, and that *tidings* meant news or a greeting arriving from somewhere else. Of all seasons, spring is the most tidal, expanding as it advances, eddying back against itself, unendingly fluid. During the runoff, when the Kennebec and Androscoggin are in spate, the current in the Bay never reverses itself—it flows steadily out, as though there were no tide at all. And yet the level of the Bay continues to fluctuate, the tide working underneath the current, raising and lowering the water level twice a day. You cannot glance at a buoy, see which way it is tilting, and tell yourself what the tide is doing. You just have to watch a piling or a stretch of shore for a while, and see whether the water is creeping up it or creeping down it. So with our springtime, so often. Judging solely from the thermometer and the daily weather, you can't confidently guess, from day to day, whether we are headed into winter or out of it. You have to trust the lengthening days, and watch and listen for the returning birds. I am qualified to say that it is possible to acquire a taste for that sort of thing, and that, once you do, every other season seems slightly enervating and insipid.

What we call spring fever is, I find, two things. One is a restlessness, an agitation that a flock of geese passing over the house at night or a pond full of peepers at dusk can suddenly trigger. Oddly, you want to go north. The other is a tendency to drop out of human time, and to sit and receive the tide of natural time as it comes at you. Each response has behind it the desire to escape from clock time and calendar time, to join, at least in imagination, the comings and goings of creatures that do not know time, but are its ancient keepers.

II

ON THE SEVENTH OF APRIL 2001, I dug a path from the back door, out around the hawthorn hedge, to the clothesline, then cleared out an area about ten feet square underneath the line. The sun was high and strong, roughly equivalent to what it would be on Labor Day. The sky was a deep and limitless blue; looking up at it gave you a kind of inverted vertigo, as though you might lose your balance and tumble, in an exalted upward somersault, into the empyrean. For all the brightness of the sun, the air felt cool and moist against the skin, the way it does when you stand above a waterfall. The snow was sublimating, turning itself directly into vapor—going straight to heaven and bypassing mud season altogether.

Two weeks later, on a Friday, I had a cup of coffee with Karen Tilberg, down at the Bowdoinham town landing. She's a lawyer and a conservationist, and a person you like to be around because she has managed to work on behalf of the things she believes in without its having diminished her love for those things. We had intended to talk over some local land use issues of mutual concern, but this was not the morning for it. We'd might as well have attempted to have an earnest discussion while the luminous veils of the aurora borealis were shifting and shimmering in the night sky, or while a blizzard was in progress. The sunlight sparkled off the river; ice floes were drifting up on the tide. Mergansers breasted the current, plunged forward to dive, bobbed back up, their fine nuptial plumage as spiffy and dry as though

Cormorant, once more abundant on the Bay

they'd just brought it back from the cleaners. On one floe, just big enough to accommodate them, stood seven cormorants, all facing the same direction. They looked rigidly solemn, uncomfortably out of place, and totally clueless, like seven pallbearers who somehow found themselves adrift on an iceberg in an arctic sea, and did not know what to do about it except go on looking as funereal as possible. An eddy brought them in close to where we were. They noticed us and started to squirm uneasily and finally launched and lumbered off, flying laboriously and just above the surface. One shat, then another, then another, as though this were a standard part of the takeoff procedure, like retracting the landing gear.

Karin was headed up north to ski that late April day, and that night I headed east toward Bangor for the Kenduskeag canoe race, which my daughter Liz and I had decided to enter that year. We think of ourselves as good canoeists, but not as racers, and the event confirmed this self-assessment— we neither won nor swam, although we came close enough on both counts to keep things interesting.

Almost the best part of the whole experience that year, and in the years that have followed, was the village of Kenduskeag at seven o'clock on a bright, calm April morning, as all the kayakers and canoeists arrived and spread themselves and their canoes out on both banks of the river, upstream of the bridge, which was the starting line. It was a friendly crowd, fraternal and sororal in the way you'd expect a crowd of pilgrims or protest marchers to be. A good many dogs were about, and small children. While their owners chatted, the dogs circled warily, sniffing as though each suspected the other of smuggling drugs, and the children, like lemmings or new-hatched turtles, toddled straight off toward the river to see if they couldn't drown themselves before anybody interfered.

Some serious paddlers were there, in aerodynamic neoprene, doing occult warm-ups or talking professionally among themselves about the best route through Six Mile Falls. But there were plenty of neophyte day trippers like me and Liz, stepping over to the Grange Hall for coffee and donuts, or doing some last minute duct-taping of wardrobe or equipment, or just gazing at the Kenduskeag. It was running high and strong, and had that clean and glittering blackness that rivers and brooks and even flowing ditches have in the spring, when everything is in spate, paddlers included.

The boats departed in groups of five, one group every minute, starting at 8:45. There were something like 478 boats, plus the dogs, children, well-wishers, spectators, officials, and a few camera-toting media personages, who tend to take up space and impede traffic. But the whole thing, possessing no outward symptoms of organization, went off smoothly; Liz and I, in canoe number 410, passed under the

Bull frog

bridge and were on our way at ten o'clock sharp.

All the way down the river, wherever it ran close to the road or somebody's yard or passed under a bridge, and especially where there were rapids, we had spectators. They had folding chairs and picnics and ice chests; some of them thriftily used the big slabs of ice left by the receding water to cool whatever needed cooling. They yelled encouragement, cracked jokes, and made themselves very much part of the fun. It had been a long winter and a late spring, with snow and more snow falling on what was already too much snow, and endemic cabin fever threatening to become epidemic at any moment. Now it was over, and here we all were; here was this bustling, bright little river and this absurd surge of people, all of them a little giddy with adrenaline, springtime, conviviality, endorphins, running water, boats jostling against each other, the sweet, plaintive overhead crying of killdeers, and other unlicensed stimulants.

Two weeks later, that in its turn was over. It hit ninety degrees on the first of May, and a drought was upon us. It took a deliberate act of memory to recall that we were still skiing in April, and worrying about ice jams and the possibility of flooding on the Kennebec.

In the middle of May, Susan and I went over to the Chewonki Foundation to attend a conference on renewable energy and energy conservation. We had decided, for a whole slew of reasons, to sell the old farmhouse and build a new house, in a woodlot we'd owned for a long time, and we needed to educate ourselves. The keynote speaker was Barry Rock, and his speech was about climate change.

It made me want to stick my head in the sand—almost any discussion of the future these days does. All of us who live here have a sort of vested interest in the Maine climate, regardless of our opinions of it. It has conditioned us to expect unexpected things, the dramas of bad weather, the temporary fulfillment of a string of idyllic mornings in May or in October, the bunker mentality of winter, the manic splurging of spring. We were told at Chewonki that a child born that very day in Boston, spending her entire life there, and having a normal life span, would die in a place that had the climate of Richmond, Virginia.

It would presumably be only a little different for her country cousin in Bowdoinham or Dresden or Bath. And the children of those children would know the meteorology of old New England only as data: that winters were five degrees colder; that summers were three degrees less hot. They will read that the sugar maple used to grow here, the brook trout and the landlocked salmon used to live in much of Maine, that the upper third of the state was covered by a huge coniferous forest, that potatoes and blueberries were raised Down East, that people used to fish through the ice on the Cathance, and drive their cars over it.

Looking across the Abby mouth toward Bath

This is hard to contemplate because it is hard to believe. And, no doubt, hard to believe because it is so hard to contemplate. That the world of seasons as we know and exult in them may be no more to our grandchildren than the meteorological data of the Wisconsin Ice Age are to us is incomprehensible—it almost severs our kinship to our descendants. Every summer erases for us the memory of the preceding winter; the first two weeks of May can make it hard to quite believe that the first two weeks of April were as they were. But now will the whole felt past of the region slip away like that—like the memory of a cold, snowy April once summer has come?

III

I HAD BEEN DOWN SOUTH FOR A WEEK at the end of March, and got back on the first Sunday in April, when we switched from standard to daylight-saving time. Even so, the newly arrived robins were singing on Monday morning by 5:00 A.M, Eastern daylight time. They are here because it is spring; it is spring because they are here. They sing because the sky is growing light; the sky grows light because they sing. No robin has ever doubted this causality. The same is true for the woodfrogs that had already begun their guttural serenade, and the peepers that were singing in desperate unison from every pond and puddle in Midcoast Maine.

Once we were less insulated than we are now from the fact that we live on a planet that rotates diurnally and orbits annually, altering our relation to the sun minute by minute and week by week. Once our own lives moved to those cyclical rhythms. Our myths and rituals and customs, our feasts and fasts and holidays still preserve vestiges of this old biological synchronicity. April comes, its rains awakening dormant vegetation in every holt and heath; in the strengthening sun and lengthening days, the birds sing fervently, right through the night, and folks from every corner of every shire in England develop a strange longing—spiritual or carnal or both—to go on a pilgrimage. That's how it was in Chaucer's world, six centuries ago. We can still feel something of their upsurge of energy and wanderlust, and share their tendency not to question it or look beyond it. It is perfectly natural to us that Chaucer's pilgrims did not remember until the very end, when they were coming down Blean Hill through the village of Harbledown and into Canterbury, that the true object of pilgrimage is not R&R but Penance.

So DAYLIGHT-SAVING TIME WENT INTO EFFECT on Sunday, the robins were singing in the predawn darkness on Monday, and the peepers were peeping in the postcrepuscular darkness of Monday night. And on the next night, at sometime around 8:45 P.M., Eastern daylight time, Pedro Martinez, out in Seattle, Washington, threw his first significant pitch of the new millenium and the new season—an unhittable and hissing fastball, outside corner. Such is his name and such is his fame that this was an event of some importance to baseball fans everywhere, but in northern New England, it marked the beginning of a narrative whose episodes are unpredictable but whose conclusion is not.

On the face of it, the Boston Red Sox are a professional baseball team. They play their games in real time, which translates into real money. Their players come from all over, and the rate of turnover among them is high. Most of them are migratory, packing their bags and leaving Boston in early October, and traveling to wintering grounds in the lower latitudes.

But a tree remains a tree even though all its leaves abandon it in the fall, and are replaced by an entirely new set in the spring. The Red Sox remain the Red Sox, a collective entity of replaceable parts, a set of apparently random and generally discordant variations on one theme. That theme is not random. It rises like upwelling sap in cities and towns and villages and lonely little isolated farms all across northern New England. It brings back the robin and awakens the peeper. It is, to give it a name, the Triumph of Hope over Experience.

Not that Hope ever really triumphs, of course—it would cease to be Hope if it did. Experience gains the upper hand every year: the peepers fade out a few voices at a time, the chorus growing more ragged and feeble as April passes; the robins sing later and less ardently. By midsummer, the grass is turning brown and things take on a tired and dusty look, as the earth tilts away from the sun.

To understand the deep and mystical connection of the Red Sox and the whole breathing and animate world, you need only read the sports pages of the *Boston Globe* and pay attention to your surroundings. In April the message from the gurus at the *Globe* and the peepers in the pond is the same. Stand beside the pond and listen to that crying that is almost painful in its urgency. Listen and hear it become language, desperate as the calling of so many men in lifeboats in the middle of the night, with the wind rising. *This year,* they say, over and over and faster and faster, *this year; thisyearthisyearthisyear.* "Pennant Fever Grips Hub" shrills the *Globe,* helplessly in the clutches of Hope.

In the same pond in July, you hear a different tune. Traditionally, bullfrogs are suppose to say *jug-o-RUM, jug-o-RUM,* a warning or invitation to drunkards. But since 1918, the last year the Sox won the World Series, they say *not-a-HOPE, not-a-HOPE.* Here and there around the fringes of the pond, a green frog answers, a single, twanging note—*NOPE. NOPE.*

There are other teams in other parts of the country, and every year one of them wins the World Series, and the citizens in that part of the country rejoice, with a vulgar jubilation that we who are said to live in New England do not really envy. The triumph of that team is mere strut and swagger, signifying nothing. The endlessly self-renewing failure of the Red Sox is an annual pageant and a myth, an acting out of the graver realities of everything that is born, lives, and dies. It is hard on the players, coaches, and fans, of course, but that's life.

I HEARD A STORY YEARS AGO, about a man many years my senior. I had just moved to Maine. The man I heard about was a lawyer from Philadelphia. All his life he had been what in Maine is known as a "sport": a rich fellow with a college education who liked to come up north for rugged recreations. In the fall, that meant hiring a guide to take him out duck hunting on Merrymeeting Bay, and in the spring it meant hiring a guide somewhere further upcountry to take him fishing for trout and landlocked salmon. He belonged to the vanished generation of men who considered a tweed jacket and a Donegal hat and knickerbockers to be recreational attire, signifying that you were in between the three-piece suit of your official existence, and the waders and fishing vest or hunting coat that you would don as a sportsman.

So he was attired that way and riding the train up to Bangor one evening in June. He would be met there by his guide and driven to the lakeside camp that was his eventual destination. A very fine, calm evening it was, and he was happy to be headed up into the North Woods again, toward the days of gentlemanly yet simple pursuits that lay ahead of him. At a stop fifteen or twenty miles west of Bangor a small, haggard-looking man got on, and, there being no other seats available, he sat down beside the lawyer. He did not return the lawyer's smile or even meet his eyes as he took his seat.

They rode stiffly on for a while, but the influence of the mild evening and his own good mood were too much for the lawyer. He felt a humane sympathy for the haggard-looking man and wished to divert him from his cares with some pleasant conversation. He turned to the man and remarked what a fine evening it was and how green and fresh everything seemed. He said how he was headed up into the North Woods and how he did that almost every spring and what a pleasure it always was to come back into the great State of Maine. The lawyer was genial, expansive, and democratic, for all the prestige of the law firm in which he was a partner and of his Main Line address and of the schools in which he had been educated. But the haggard-looking man did not thaw, or show any sign of hearing him at all. The lawyer attributed this to rustic shyness, and was determined to overcome it.

"And tell me, sir," he said, "where might *you* be headed this evening?"

The haggard man responded with the vehement and pent finality of a trap snapping shut:

"I am going to *Bangor* to git *drunk*, and God do I dread it."

I liked that story the first time I heard it, and I like it better with every year that passes. The peepers peep *thisyearthisyearthisyear*, the umpire calls out *play ball*, the conductor cries *all aboard.* Against our better wisdom, foreknowing the outcome, we clamber on, and ride the bittersweet promise of springtime towards its inevitable outcome.

Note: Yes, the Red Sox won the pennant in 2004, and then the World Series, dispatching the Yankees and the Cardinals, two of their ancient nemeses, in the process. The consequences of this breach of mythic protocol remain to be seen: it may be the clearest indication yet of the regional impact of global warming. At the other extreme, it may simply have been the sort of aberration that ultimately confirms the norm. Losing would lose its bittersweetness and its sorrow if it were not, every fourscore and six years or so, whetted, refreshed, and reinvigorated by victory.

IV

FOR AS LONG AS WE LIVED IN THE OLD FARMHOUSE, surrounded by pastures, we watched and waited for the arrival of bobolinks. They showed up with great consistency, on or about the ides of May, ten days or so before the lilacs bloomed. To us they were the primary sponsors, celebrants, and incarnations of Springtime Triumphant.

They belong to the troupials, a family of affiliated species occurring only in the New World, and including blackbirds, orioles, and meadowlarks. If you live, as we did, around the right sort of habitat, anywhere from Pennsylvania up into the Maritime Provinces and as far west as the Great Lakes, you cannot possibly miss the bobolinks when they return to their nesting territories; if you don't, you may go to your grave without seeing one.

Their closest allies are farmers; so are their worst enemies. The better the farmer, the worse, from a bobolink's point of view. If he is farsighted, prosperous, and on top of things—the kind who keeps his pastures well fertilized, ploughs and re-seeds every five years or so, and gets two cuttings of prime hay off them per summer, he is an unworthy steward of his acres, a public enemy. But if he belongs to that undervalued class of people who operate at suboptimal efficiency, are always behind and always too busy catching up to last week to think about next year, then he is their friend, their patron saint, and their salvation. He does not get around to haying until August, and so their nests and fledglings are spared. He does not re-seed or fertilize with much regularity, and his fields reward him with poor hay, vetch, buttercups, hawkweed, asters, fragrant bedstraw, and blue-eyed grass. And, best of all, with bobolinks. Studies show that they prefer "old" fields—ones that have gone eight years or more since the last re-seeding, and that are comparatively sparse and weedy.

Of course if the farmer succumbs entirely to apathy, despair, poor returns, goldenrod, milkweed, thistles, and eventually to alders and poplars and pines—if he stops mowing altogether—then the bobolinks desert him. They grace with their presence those whose labor is honorable, sincere, always hoping for success and never achieving it, is both never-ending and an end in itself. The Red Sox might consider renaming themselves the Bobolinks, and letting the grass grow long in the outfield.

Before the Europeans with their axes and oxen and grasses arrived, bobolinks were primarily a Midwestern species. As the Europeans pushed westward, transforming the landscape, the bobolinks pushed east, colonizing the pastures and meadows that were now available to them. It is a good thing that they did—the plough would deprive them of most of the Midwestern grasslands that had been their primary breeding grounds. Thus, like such birds as barn swallows, chimney swifts, and purple martins, they are now both wild and domestic, as dependent on us as horses or housecats, but still as free as ever in their comings and goings. They assert their independence in late July and August, when they leave us behind and set out for their wintering grounds in northern Argentina. This seems to be the longest migration made by any New World songbird, although several shorebirds and waterfowl outdo it.

In mid-May, the males show up in small gangs of six or eight. They will all nest in the same general area—the same hayfield, for example—and compete for territory and females among themselves. They will share a common musical dialect, and pass it on to their sons. They will leave for Argentina at the same time. And if all goes well, they will return back to the same place at the same time next year.

You could as easily overlook the arrival of a gang of motorcyclists or presidential candidates. They believe in advertising their presence and playing to the crowd, even if the crowd is imaginary. They are black below and white or buffy above, like an upside-down penguin. This is an eye-catchingly heterodox fashion statement. Most birds, mammals, reptiles, and fish are countershaded: darker on the back, paler on the belly. Thus the shadow on the critter's underside is offset by the paleness there, making the whole animal less noticeable. That, for example, is why deer standing in a field are so easily overlooked and why, when you do see them, they appear insubstantial, as though sculpted out of smoke.

But the whole point of being a male bobolink is to stand out, to be noticed. He perches on wires, on the very tips of shrubs, or teeters on the stems of tall grasses. He sings there. He also sings in flight, flying with his head thrown back, his tail angled downward, and his wings in a trembling flutter, as though he had held them stiffly out to the side and induced some sort of seizure or convulsive spasm in himself. He returns to the ground with his wings locked in a vee above him, in a guided free fall like the winged seed of a maple, still singing as he descends. The song is burbling, effervescent, ecstatic. If you are looking for modest, dignified self-restraint, the eloquent sincerity of understatement, look elsewhere. This bird is not merely full of himself. He is overflowing with himself; he is *stylin'*. And he does not, like the woodcock, put on his bravura performance in the chaste seclusion of the late evening hours. He's a prime-time performer, hard at it right through the middle of the day.

For the first four or five days after they return to their breeding grounds, the males claim their territories and chase each other—and just about any other bird this side of a Cooper's hawk—off them. Then the females—noticeably smaller than the males, and as inconspicuous and nondescript in their plumage as sparrows—arrive, and the males add them to the list of things that need chasing. These chases are prolonged and low, right across the tops of the grasses, the male a foot or two behind the female, following her swerve for swerve, a model for fighter pilots everywhere. Life seems to be a nonstop lark, except that the bobolink outlarks all the larks that have ever larked anywhere on the earth. It should surprise and scandalize no one to learn that the males are ardently polygamous. But not heartless. The

male participates fully in the brooding and feeding of the family of his first mate, but does not leave his subsequent families entirely in the lurch. He provides a sort of domestic triage to them, helping the females most urgently in need of it. So he is not a deadbeat dad, although surely, by the end of the nesting season, a dad that is dead beat.

Somewhere in early to mid-July, a kind of magic goes out of the world. The grass and leaves lose the vivid freshness of their first emergence, the streams and rivers settle into a sluggish serenity, the birds sing less often, less ardently, and less early. The Red Sox drop out of first place and start to squabble with the press, the owners, and each other. Tourists clog the roads and beaches, and even blackflies and mosquitoes go into a funk. At about this time, the male bobolinks begin to look bedraggled, and then seem to disappear because they have molted and assumed the undistinguished appearance of the females and the young of the year. It is sad, with that particular kind of sadness of the latter part of the summer: beautiful weather, few insects, but also the sense that the unlimited possibilities of another spring have withered back into finitude.

The one place where this is not true is the Bay, where the wild rice is beginning to assume its full stature and the grains are beginning to form. In the lives of bobolinks in eastern North America, this is not an insignificant coincidence. Migration is fueled by fat, and the bobolink, with its astonishingly long annual itinerary, needs a lot of it. Rice, wild and domestic, is a rich source, and so they change their diets, and go from being primarily insectivorous to being herbivorous and more particularly, to being *oryzivorous*—rice-eating. This dietary preference is so pronounced that it gives them half of their official name—*Dolichonyx* (long-toed) *oryzivorous*. I have the impression that rice is less important to them up here than it is as they move south. When there were big stands of wild rice along the lower Delaware and Potomac Rivers, southbound bobolinks descended on them in vast numbers in the late summer.

But their reputation as rice-eaters really came from further south than that, and especially from the South Carolina lowcountry, where the cultivation of domestic rice had begun early in the colonial period, and had, by the nineteenth century, transformed most of the original lowland swamps into vast plantations, with diked fields that could be flooded during the growing season and then drained and dried out for harvest in the early fall. By all accounts, the bobolinks blitzed them by the millions then, and they were regarded as a sort of locust with feathers, capable of destroying the whole crop if left to their own devices. They were shot from dawn until dark, and since they, unlike locusts, were highly edible, the fat little birds were collected and shipped off to northern markets or consumed locally. The Civil War put an end to large-scale rice cultivation in the Carolina lowcountry, but when I

was growing up there bobolinks were still generally referred to as ricebirds, and were not regarded with affection. Two hundred years ago, they may have been the only sentient creature on the continent to approve equally of the dour and thrifty farmers of New England and the lordly oligarchs— among the very wealthiest and most undemocratic citizens of North America—of the Carolina lowcountry. When rice stopped being grown along the South Atlantic seaboard, the bobolink population nosedived, and it has never recovered its once staggering abundance. All the same, when I used to duck hunt in those old rice fields, which had long since reverted to marsh, large flocks of them would fly overhead in the evenings, making a metallic kind of plinking noise.

Until I came to Maine, I had never seen a male in its breeding plumage, seen its antics, or heard its song. In the chilly, blustery weather of the springs that I had not yet learned to relish and yearn for, the bobolinks were something totally unexpected—a troupe of harlequins suddenly showing up in the front yard and the unkempt pastures around it. The bird life of South Carolina was and is more diversified, more numerous, and more constant than that of Maine—down there, you wake up to the sound of something singing or calling every day of the year. Yet it had nothing quite so sassy and showy as this. It gradually began to dawn on me that, whether in Maine, South Carolina, or some other state, many of the birds we think of as "ours," are only tourists, up from the tropics. And I reckoned that a higher percentage of the birds that summered and bred in Maine were tropical than of the birds that summered and bred in South Carolina—or at any rate, these visitors were more essentially and conspicuously a part of what made Maine's summer summer.

Bobolink migration, like all bird migration, remains in many particulars mysterious, but because of its unusual length, it has been studied with unusual care. We now know that iron oxides in the vicinity of the bobolink's nasal opening are reactive to the earth's magnetic field and provide the bird with a kind of compass, which plays an especially large role in its navigational system. It also relies on the configurations of the stars in the night sky to tell it when to leave and how to recognize its latitude and set its course. They arrive in Argentina for a second summer, and, while there, feed chiefly on crops and are persecuted accordingly. If they went only a little further south in Argentina, they would begin to experience the longer hours of daylight that apparently trigger their mating behavior, and so they would have no need to make the great long journey that brings them back to Bowdoinham in May. Why and how did all of this evolve? Surely it would have made more sense for them to go a little further south and stay put, or, failing that, to migrate southward instead of northward, and so cut their mileage and avoid the dangerous leg of their flight that carries them across the Gulf of Mexico.

Here in Bowdoinham, still a town with a good scattering of derelict barns and old pastures and other remnants of an agricultural past, we might as well take a shortsighted, solipsistic, and self-congratulatory view of the matter. They return here to tell us that we are living right, keeping our lives, if not our bank accounts, balanced; they return here because our notorious springs (they know no winters—only springs, summers, and falls) are what they dream about, down there in the pampas.

Young snapper, September

Voices of the Turtle

W<small>E WERE HAVING A PICNIC UNDER THE BIG PINES</small> down at the end of Wildes Point, looking out over the marshes of the Cathance delta. It was late August, late afternoon. The sun lit up Pleasant Point, Center Point, and Brick Island, but it was cool in the shadows where we were, and you could feel the summer beginning to drain away. Tight little swarms of blackbirds were feeding in the rice. The tide had just begun to push back into the guzzles and seep out toward the flats and the grass.

As we came down to the point, we'd noticed an unfamiliar pick-up parked some ways up from the water: three-quarter ton, with a homemade camper on the back of it. The camper was of the oversized sort that projects forward over the cab of the truck, and that aspires to make an honest pickup into something like an RV. But this one didn't have that effect at all: it had no windows, was made of unpainted plywood, and had a grim, rough-and-ready look about it. The door over the tailgate was secured with a heavy hasp and a big padlock, so we assumed that the owner was not inside. We had speculated about who he might be, where he might be, and what he might be up to: transporting drugs? illegal aliens? stolen property? short lobsters? But then we'd forgotten about him, settled down to our picnic, built ourselves a small fire against the evening chill, and watched the shadows stretch out across the marsh, the tide gradually overflowing the channels and guzzles, and creeping up the shore below us.

We'd just doused the fire and were gathering up our things when the truck's owner showed up, paddling a canoe. He pulled in just below us, got out, and we said hello. He said hello back, picked a burlap sack up out of the canoe, and went up toward the truck, the sack—obviously heavy—in one hand and his paddle in the other. He resembled his vehicle—grim, rough-and-ready, and with something about him that so obviously discouraged curiosity that it made you all the more curious. Susan, to be friendly, remarked that it was a nice evening. He turned around, looked back out over the Bay, and considered:

"I suppose it is," he said, turned back, and went on up the hill.

He returned to get his canoe. He was a big man and lifted it easily, carried it up, and was tying it down as we walked out past the truck. The camper door was now open, and what I saw inside it surprised me—the interior appeared to be entirely taken up with shelves, each basically a sheet of plywood that stretched from wall to wall and from the rear of the truck all the way up to the cab. They were spaced a

foot or so apart. He saw me looking, and asked if I'd like to see what he had inside. I said I would, and he reached into his pocket, extracted a small flashlight, and shined it into the interior. The beam wasn't strong. I could make out dim, lumpy shapes, most of them up toward the cab, scrabbling in a ponderous, aimless way that suggested a kind of numbed despair. One lifted its head and the light caught its beady eye, and threw the shadow of the head against the back wall of the camper, and I could see what I was looking at—two dozen or so snapping turtles, with more presumably on the shelves above.

That is how I met John Rogers, interstate trapper and wholesaler of snapping turtles. We talked for half an hour or so. He spoke deliberately and with the pardonable dogmatism of a man who spends a great deal of time by himself, knows and cares a great deal about something that most people know nothing about, and, when he undertakes to explain what he does for a living, regularly encounters something between disbelief and amusement. He was tall, raw-boned, and bearded, and he spoke well, so that it was satisfying to listen to him, although his tone, while not exactly aggressive, implied some sort of ingrained contrariness, as though he expected disagreement or disapproval. He seemed like an anachronism, even by my standards—a throwback to an earlier America, the world of the pioneer, river rat, mountain man, prospector: the bunch-quitter who carried individualism and independence to their extreme limits in the unsettled hinterlands and inhospitable backwaters of a nation that once had had plenty of both.

People who live outside of town or at the edge of town, almost anywhere east of the Rockies, have probably encountered a snapper or two, and almost always in the same circumstance: as a big, blatant, hissing, snapping, lunging intruder into their backyards or along their roadsides. These encounters happen in late spring or early summer, when the females come up out of the rivers, swamps, ponds, mires, bogs, ditches, or fens to find a sandy spot, dig their nests, and lay their eggs. Otherwise, snappers are pretty much invisible, which makes their annual emergence seem mysterious and a little sinister, as though once a year, they were sent forth from the underworld, a space ship, or the unconscious mind to remind us, à la Stephen King, of a general ghastly ghoulishness woven into the web of the everyday world. Dogs bark at them; boys may tease or torment them—they are manifestly formidable, and at the same time largely helpless. An early encounter with a snapper may be decisive in turning a child toward a fascination with critters of all sorts, or in giving the child a lifelong aversion to wild animals in general, and cold-blooded ones in particular. They don't have the aspect of elderly benignity that we associate with turtles, and evoke instead something of the same fear and attraction

that snakes do, as is suggested by their scientific name: *Chelydra serpentina serpentina*.

We fill in our ignorance with our imaginations, and so there is a considerable folklore around snappers—if one ever latches onto you, it will hold on until it thunders, even if you cut off its head; if you wade unwarily into a pond, one may catch you by the toe and if you holler, won't let go—it'll slowly pull you under, inexorable as quicksand; its jaws can crush broomsticks or bones; and so forth. I had outgrown that sort of lurid mythology, but hadn't replaced it with much information. John Rogers told me a lot of things I did not know—that snappers are primarily herbivores, for example, and that his pursuit of them took him as far south as Georgia and as far west and north as the multitudinous lakes along the Ontario–Manitoba border. He said the market for them now was chiefly urban and predominantly Midwestern. Relocated black Southerners, emigrants from Appalachia, and Catholics were his most reliable customers. The pope, he said, deemed turtles to be a species of fish, and so a permissible food on Fridays and during Lent. As a general proposition, people's fondness for snappers declined as their respectability increased. He pronounced *respectability* with an unfriendly emphasis, as though to indicate that he regarded it as one thing, and self-respect, which he showed no signs of lacking, as more or less its opposite.

Most snappers in Maine were smaller than the ones a little further south, averaging about twenty pounds apiece, although some got bigger than that. His personal best came from Massachusetts—sixty-seven pounds. In Georgia and the Carolinas, they were smaller than in New England, on average. In calm weather on one of his favorite clear, shallow lakes of Ontario, he could lean over the side of his canoe and watch snappers walking across the bottom, raising a cloud of mud.

"I used to wonder how they catch so many fish, but that showed me. Shiners get drawn to all that mud, and whatever gets stirred up in it. They swarm around those turtles, and sometimes the turtle stops, so that he's right in the middle of the mud-cloud. The fish don't worry about him—a turtle's big and slow, like a tank, and a fish is little and quick, like a kid on a motor scooter. What the fish don't know"— and he suddenly thrust his hand toward my face, snapping it shut an inch or so from my nose—"is that if it's a tank, it's got a *gun*."

When I tried to get down to particulars about how he caught his turtles, and how he recognized good turtle water, he got cagy. He said he often didn't bother with traps, and that he found turtles by keeping his eyes open and knowing where to look and what to look for. The Bay had a lot of turtles in it, but because it was so big, they weren't concentrated, and you had to do a fair amount of paddling for every one you caught.

I had the feeling that he was in no hurry, and that he shared with more ordinary people—college professors for example—the pleasure of imparting information to an eager and attentive audience. But the audience, alas, had some chore to do or errand to run, and needed to get back to the schedules of life. So I said good-bye, and that I was glad to have met him. He said if I wanted to know more about him, I should get my hands on a copy of *Yankee Magazine*, written a year or two ago. There was an article in there about him, and he thought it wasn't bad.

I eventually found the article: "King of the Snappers," by Richard Conniff, in the June 1989 edition of *Yankee Magazine*. Conniff tells how he had for years heard about a legendary turtle trapper. Finally an ecologist at Bard College, who was studying snappers, mentioned someone he'd worked with who fit that description. His name was Jasz Rodziewicz, but he was now generally known to people as John Rogers. The ecologist said Rodziewicz-Rogers had a knowledge of the haunts and habits of snapping turtles that seemed to exceed that of the entire scientific community. He did not know how to get in touch with him, but did know that Rogers spent his winters in northern Maine, where he had a cabin and ran a trapline.

The ecologist and others led Conniff to expect a man who was a bit uncanny in his ability to pull turtles out of a pond the way a magician pulls rabbits out of a hat, and more than a bit offish, secretive, and hard to find. But Conniff persisted, and eventually tracked down and interviewed John Rogers at his cabin in Maine, in midwinter. They talked from dark until well past midnight, while Rogers was skinning out and stretching onto frames a day's worth of mink and muskrat. The essay that emerged from this conversation is good, substantially more than the usual sort of "my-most-unforgettable-character" piece.

Jasz Rodziewicz, as he then was, was born and grew up in the 1940s in northern New Jersey. His family improvised a living—trucking, small-scale farming, and freelance foraging for whatever could be caught or killed, eaten or sold, in the upper Delaware valley. He caught his first snapper when he was nine; a kinsman sold it to a fish market for a dollar, which was what young Jasz earned for a day's labor on his uncle's farm. It was no contest; he caught twenty-eight more turtles that summer.

Rogers went to NYU and did some graduate work in European history at Columbia before realizing that was wasting his time—he had already found his life's vocation. He turned pro and made himself into a formidable and ruthless businessman. Whenever he got wind of another turtle-trapper, he made it his business to move in on that man's territory and more or less clean it out, making sure, as he did so, that his competitor understood why the supply had suddenly dried up. He reckoned he had put eight or ten rivals entirely

Survivor

Destroyed snapper nest. Raccoons are the probable culprit.

out of business. Others were permitted to continue, but only within a drastically reduced field of operations. That was one side of him—he was the Don Corleone of a business that, one assumes, the IRS chooses to ignore.

The other side was very different. Turtles were a commodity to him, but they were also the objects of a passion that was mystical, intellectual, and unflagging. He might have a ton and a half of snappers in his truck, ready to go to market. He could pull out any one, look at it, and tell where he had caught it. And he could look at any body of water that was new to him, and predict what subtle features of coloration and growth rate would distinguish its snappers. They were to him what rocks are to geologists, lumps of encoded information. But they were also something else. In his travels, he slept in the cab of his truck, with the back full of turtles. "When I wake up at night, I can tell what time it is by how the turtles are. The hissing and scratching and the sound of their claws, and the shells rubbing together. That's how close I get to them. I feel I could come back as a snapping turtle and be happy.... I spend the whole week with turtles. It's just me and them, me and the snappers against the world. And then what do I do? I take 'em into the cities and the suburbs and I sell 'em. I'm selling my friends. Every Thursday night I spend selling. At the end of the night, the truck's going to be empty and I'll be alone again."

He had for a long time undertaken, as Conniff puts it, to do "penance for his transgressions against the Great Turtle." He had learned how to incubate snapper eggs, and when they hatched he kept the turtles in a local pond until they weighed four pounds or so. Then he recaptured them, put them into his truck, and stocked them in likely places. He favored newly built ponds of the sort that are created as ornaments for swanky housing developments or water hazards on golf courses. He did his stocking under the cover of darkness. When Conniff interviewed him, he had been at his trade for twenty-six years, in which time he had caught, transported, and sold 84,000 turtles. And in which time, he estimated, he had stocked a quarter of a million of them. He considered that the national snapping turtle population was at or near an all-time high, because of all the small, manmade ponds—ideal habitat—that had been created in their range. He never kept a turtle that weighed less than ten pounds or more than fifty-three. The ecologist who had worked with him said he could glance at a turtle and know its weight to within a few ounces.

He had returned the sixty-seven-pound one, a male, to the Massachusetts pond it came from, after he'd had it officially weighed. As far as he knew, it was still there. He hoped so. While he was handling it, he got a feeling for its personality; he found it "rather nonchalant and lackadaisical about me after the first few snaps. I came to like him."

I DIDN'T THINK ABOUT JOHN ROGERS AGAIN until one night ten or twelve years later. The Friends of Merrymeeting Bay runs a regular monthly lecture series, and the organization has been remarkably successful in finding speakers who have authority in matters of policy, history, and natural history that directly or indirectly pertain to the Bay. On this occasion, the speaker was a woman I'd never heard of, and her subject was snapping turtles. It was a wet, warmish night, and I drove over to Dresden, where the meeting would be held in the library of the Bridge Academy. I got there early enough to help set up folding chairs for the audience; somebody else was rigging up a slide projector and a screen.

The speaker arrived. She was attractively fit, dressed in the casual, practical way you'd dress if you were going to do some light yard work, and she looked very little older than the students I taught at Bowdoin. We'd been told that she came from Machias, but when she spoke, her accent was from a good deal further east than that—from Germany, as it would turn out. She was one of those casually charismatic people who manage to seem both completely at ease in speaking to a group, and at the same time completely ingenuous. She carried a box containing the slides for that evening. Coming along behind her, two somewhat bemused FOMB volunteers carried between them a washtub, from which scratching noises emerged. They set it down on the floor beside the podium.

She introduced herself—Susanne Kynast—and told us that she had come from Germany to get an undergraduate degree from the University of Maine at Machias. UMM sponsored orientation trips for entering students, and she'd gone on one, a canoeing and camping expedition on nearby waters. Among the unfamiliar things she'd seen there was a snapping turtle, which seemed to her a remarkable creature. Nobody could tell her much about it that she couldn't see for herself: it was an aquatic turtle with an exceptionally long neck—almost as long as the shell, when fully extended—a skimpy undershell, or plastron—and a generally prehistoric look about it. Her classmates told her the usual scare stories about the fearsome power of the jaws and the danger of swimming in waters where turtles were present, but nobody seemed to know or care much about what the turtles actually ate, how they reproduced, overwintered, and otherwise kept themselves in business.

She went on to tell us a good deal that she had found out, both by reading and through her own fieldwork. At some point, fairly early into what had until then been a solidly informative talk, she leaned over and lifted a good-sized snapper out of the washtub—an adult female, she said—and held it as she talked to us. She cradled it, right-side up, in the crook of her arm. To demonstrate its harmlessness, she leaned her face down to it, nuzzling it. Then she handed it to the chairperson of the Friends of Merrymeeting Bay, Ed Friedman, and asked him to start passing it through the audience. For a moment, Ed—on the one hand, not wanting to be unobliging to a guest speaker, especially to so attractive and winning a one as this, and on the other hand, considering what liability issues might be involved—hesitated. But the turtle, when he took it, seemed harmless enough, if not exactly happy, and so he handed it down to somebody on the front row, and it was passed from there through the room, like a collection plate or a sign-up sheet. While this was going on, Susanne Kynast took three other snappers from the washtub and set them on the floor. They set off purposefully in three different directions. Then she returned to her talk.

On the smooth floor, the at-large turtles did not move so energetically as they normally do on land—they could get no traction, and their feet kept slipping out from under them. The collection-plate turtle kept up a steady swimming motion as it passed from one pair of hands to the next. This did not suggest fright or aggression so much as preoccupation, as though the turtle needed to get somewhere, and could not understand why its usual method of locomotion wasn't working. From time to time, one of the at-large turtles would get itself into a corner, where it kept right on pushing ahead, going nowhere, until someone got up, went over, and turned it in another direction. Twice a turtle got caught up in

the extension cord to the projector and kept going, pulling the plug out of the socket and causing a temporary blackout. All in all they seemed mild, clueless, and hapless, with not much going for them except their ferocious ugliness, and now even that was being called into question—two little girls behind me were asking their mother PLEASE could they take one home? THEY would feed it and look after it—PROMISE.

It did not surprise me to learn from Susanne Kynst that snapping turtles grow slowly, and do not reach sexual maturity until they are about twenty years old; or that the average age for a breeding female is over thirty years. And it did not surprise me to learn that a lot of females are killed on the highway, or that the eggs are frequently dug up by raccoons, skunks, and foxes. And it did not surprise me to learn that snappers, if they survive their first three or four years, have very few natural enemies. She said that no more than a half of I percent of the eggs laid by a female would hatch into turtles that survived to maturity. That would still be enough to sustain the population, since her career might easily last for fifty years, during which she would lay many hundreds of eggs.

Snappers, or turtles very much like them, have been around for eons; they were busily minding their own business when the dinosaurs evolved, and when the dinosaurs vanished. But Susanne Kynast thought that we should now begin to worry about them and their future. Through most of their range, and particularly in Maine, where good nesting habitat is hard to come by, they now migrate straight into the enclaves of humanity every June, when time comes for them to lay their eggs. They need well-drained, sandy soil that is close to water, and they find it around bridge abutments and the causeways leading up to them, or along the shoulders of highways, or in small, earthen dams. This has the effect of making them into communal nesters, and it greatly simplifies the job of predators. In a couple of nights along the edge of a good stretch of road, a raccoon can wipe out an entire generation of turtles from a fair-sized pond or drainage. Even if it happens to overlook an egg or two, its having disrupted the nest guarantees that no hatchlings will emerge.

Given the longevity of snappers—their life expectancy exceeds ours, once they attain maturity, and, unlike us, they steadily increase in size and reproductive capacity as they get older—an increase in hatchling mortality would not in itself endanger the species. The great risk that we pose to them has to do with the number of mature females that are killed every year. If the female were *very* mature—sixty or seventy years old, for example—the odds might favor her having already been responsible for two or more turtles that had themselves grown to maturity. But if she were relatively young—still in her first decade of productive existence—the odds would run the other way. Susanne Kynast did not overstate her case—her point was that the survival strategy of

snapping turtles, which had served them well enough over a staggering period of time, might now be working against them, given the current mortality rate in the breeding population. There was only so much we could do—we could educate people, and encourage them to see the turtles for what they are; we could try to protect nests against predation, although that would be difficult. And, at the very least, we could outlaw the commercial harvesting of turtles. At present, it did not amount to a great deal, because demand was low in this country. But elsewhere, and particularly in China, turtles were highly esteemed as a food, and brought fancy prices. It was only a matter of time until the global demand discovered our local supply, and when it did, turtle trapping would become a lucrative business.

Even leaving aside the things that made turtles uniquely vulnerable, her reasoning had the authority of history behind it. A few decades of high prices for caviar had left us with only a vestige of our native sturgeon population; the same thing, it appeared, might now be happening with eels. And it had happened over and over again with fish and wildlife populations that had once seemed inexhaustible. In one of the more unlikely grass-roots campaigns I've ever seen or heard of, Susanne Kynast would go on to build a coalition, put the issue before the Maine Department of Inland Fisheries and Wildlife, and, within a year, succeed in getting

Female snapper, June

Camera shy

commercial turtle trapping banned in Maine. At the time she did so, only five citizens of the state held commercial turtle-trapping licenses, and only one of them, John Rogers, appeared to testify on behalf of the industry at a public hearing. He felt the department's action was hasty, founded more on sentiment than on science, and unjust to people like himself, simply because they were not a wealthy or vocal constituency. From his remarks, as reported by Phyllis Austin in the *Maine Environmental News* (July 26, 2002), it appeared that he had read Susan Kynast's work carefully, and by and large admired it, and that they'd had mutually respectful and informative conversations about snappers. But her research, centered in Washington County and spanning only a few years, was hardly comparable to his experience of more than fifty years, in Maine and all across North America.

He considered that Maine's snappers were not big enough, and their populations weren't concentrated enough, for them to attract a significant number of trappers. That appeared to make his argument somewhat self-contradic-tory—on the one hand, commercial turtle harvesting should be allowed in the state; on the other hand, there weren't enough big ones here to make it worthwhile. That seemed consistent with my memory of him—a man from the heroic age of American individualism, with a spirit of contradiction that might from time to time lead him to con-tradict himself, given his fine, Emersonian contempt for small consistencies and the hobgoblins of petty minds.

In ADDITION TO WAITING ON THE EMERGENCE of the snap-pers every spring, as one of those seasonal events that is both reassuring and surprising, I have taken to looking more care-fully for them around the Bay. In midsummer, paddling in the tidal portion of the Cathance and poking up into the mucky creeks that drain into it, Susan and I have learned to watch for agitated clumps of bullrush or pickerel weed, or simply for a line of air bubbles coming up from the bottom. Once we came on one rooting around very vigorously, churn-ing up the water to such an extent that it was invisible until we were within a yard of it, when it bobbed to the surface and raised its head. From what I have learned, it was in all probability a male, because males, not being exposed to auto-mobiles and other hazards of civilization, generally live longer and get bigger. His head was perhaps as big as a base-ball, and from what I have learned, I am sure that he weighed no more than thirty or forty pounds. And I am sure from all that I have learned that he was utterly harmless. If I had not learned all that I have learned, I would have said that his head was the size of a grapefruit, and his carapace the size of a washtub, that he weighed not less than fifty pounds, and that his beady eyes were full of misanthropic menace. Susan had not learned all that I had learned, and backpaddled vig-orously. She had been listening to Seamus Heaney reading aloud from his translation of *Beowulf,* and perhaps Grendel, the dark ogre from the fens, who crawls up into the illuminated world of men and wreaks havoc there, was in her mind. And, for all that I had learned, I could not entirely separate myself from her reaction. There is a quality of reverence in certain kinds of fear, and they become matters of faith.

The best time to see snappers around the Bay seems to be when the water is rising, and they, like the carp, begin to move out over the mudflats or—since they sometimes simply bury themselves on low tide—to emerge from them. A windless day is best, so that you can detect small disturbances in the marsh, or faint ripples on the surface. They do not inhabit deep water, and they do not swim, except when absolutely necessary, and then only for short distances. Occasionally you will see one, caught by the receding tide, walking across the mud to get itself back to water. It is very unusual indeed to see one basking—that has happened to me only once, on the Machias River, in May, when the water was still very cold. That was another big one, and he had hauled himself up onto a surprisingly steep rock in the middle of the stream. The sun had dried him thoroughly, and the algae that covered his shell was a slightly luminous lime green, which made him look like he'd consulted the wrong wardrobe consultant.

Heather's photographs were taken at the Muddy River bridge, which either affords the best nesting territory, or is adjacent to the best turtle habitat, of any place around the Bay—dozens of females haul out and dig their nests there every June. I particularly like her image of a young one that has reached the water. It has by no means left all danger behind it; the odds will not favor its survival until it has lived three or four more years. There are herons, mink, otters, stripers out there. But it is in its primal element now, moving with a new speed and ease. It looks like any ungainly young creature, still unfamiliar with the means of locomotion with which it is to undertake its perilous journey through life, and it looks as ancient as anything on earth, and it is both those things.

Caution

Juvenile eagle, Bluff Head

Sowango

Swan Island apparently owes its name to one bird and in fact owes it to another. It's an amputated Anglicization of the Abenaki *sownago*—eagle. Charlie Todd, the state's premier eagle biologist, has identified more than seventy islands, ponds, points, and lakes in Maine that incorporate *swan* in their names. All must have been places where eagles were exceptionally plentiful—communal roosts, shorelines where they concentrated when fish were running, or prime nesting habitat. Places like that existed up and down both coasts of North America, particularly around estuaries, and also around and along many inland waters. They still exist in Alaska, where hundreds and even thousands of eagles may congregate to overwinter, or to feast on spawning salmon.

In general, eagles like big water because they like fish, which almost always make up the greater part of their diet. But systematic observation by ornithologists indicates that they aren't particularly good at catching them. Shallow water helps, and they are more likely to watch for fish from an inshore perch than to seek them by soaring over open water, as an osprey does. Enormous concentrations of fish— anadromous fish or lake fish moving up into tributaries to spawn—also help, but such concentrations no longer occur in the Lower Forty-eight on anything like the scale that they once did.

So eagles fish, but rather ineptly. They also eat carrion, but how many times do you see an eagle, in Maine or elsewhere, feeding on roadside carrion? Crows, vultures, ravens, yes. Once in a great while a red-tailed hawk. But eagles? Never in my life. And they will rob or confiscate the kills of other predators—ospreys most commonly, but also hawks, foxes, and other eagles. In my observation, their success with ospreys is by no means assured—an osprey carrying a small fish may outmaneuver an eagle, and it sometimes drops a larger fish that still has enough life in it to dive and disappear when it hits the water.

Leave aside, then, the fact that they were shot, trapped, and deliberately poisoned for a century and a half after having been designated our national bird, and that indirect poisoning—by pesticides, industrial pollution, and the lead shot which they ingested from dead or crippled game—turned much of their everyday food into a malignancy, undermining their metabolic and reproductive processes. Even without that, the question is how do eagles manage to feed themselves, here around the Bay and elsewhere in the Lower Forty-eight? The answer isn't remotely apparent to me, but it must be to the eagles. Whenever you go out onto the Bay, you will most likely see the evidence of their success—the bird itself—glaring down at you from a big pine on Bluff Head, peering over the rim of a nest on Freyer Island, or soaring above the Eastern River marshes.

For a few years, the Department of Inland Fisheries and Wildlife, apparently sharing my perception, put road-killed deer out on the ice, thinking that a regular food supply would enable more birds to survive the winter, and that this, in turn, would boost the statewide population. But while the carcasses did serve to concentrate overwintering eagles, and provided good eagle-watching opportunities, they seem to have had no overall effect. The state's population continued to increase at about 7 percent a year. And recent studies have indicated that, once a bald eagle is fully fledged and has left the nest, the odds are in its favor. In one study, nearly 75 percent of juvenile birds survived to their first birthday, and in another it was a full 100 percent. Most raptors experience high mortality in the first year—for example, fewer than 50 percent of young ospreys can expect to live through it. For all raptors, survival rates improve thereafter, but here, too, eagles have the edge.

By bird standards they live a long time—fifteen or twenty years. They mate for life, but do not rush into it, attaining sexual maturity only in their fifth or sixth year. Of creatures around the Bay, perhaps only human beings postpone their entry into maturity and monogamy (assuming, in the face of substantial evidence to the contrary, that our achievement of the one automatically coincides with the achievement of the other) for a proportionately long time. Once paired off, they build or take over a nest, and get down to perpetuating the species.

A chick hatched in May is fully grown and on its own by October. In terms of wingspan and body length, the juvenile bird at this point is actually somewhat larger than an adult eagle of the same sex. In its first year of life, the eagle is solidly dark, with no white showing on the head, tail, chest, belly, and back, and only a little apparent on the underside of the wings. The eye and beak are also dark. By the next year, the bird at a distance still looks dark all over, but through binoculars or at closer range it reveals an erratic streaking on the underside, as though it had been spattered with bleach or whitewash. The beak begins to show some yellow. Within the next year and a half, the tail gradually turns white, and white feathers begin to appear in the head.

Bald eagles in Maine fully assume their iconic plumage when they are five or six years old. Seen from above or below, the body and wings are uniformly darker than at any point in their immaturity, the head, neck, and tail are a pure and lusterless white, the eyes pale, and the beak solid yellow. The clean, sharp contrasts give the adult bird a look of imposing formality—the younger bird is to it as a soldier in combat fatigues is to the same soldier in dress uniform, its menace and power now sheathed in a tautly tailored elegance.

In Bowdoinham at present, you may chance to see an eagle at about any time of the day and the year, simply in the course of going about your routines—walking down to the mailbox, commuting to work, or whatever. It happens just frequently enough and just infrequently enough to make you feel that a degree of wildness still frames our domesticity, and one of this continent's alpha predators from time to time finds it worthwhile to drift over our backyards and houses. But the Bay is the place to see them in their own backyards, going about their own routines.

I'm out on the Bay a lot more in the fall—from September until the coves begin to freeze over, usually in early December—than at any other time of year. The young birds are fully fledged by then and flying confidently. Their parents, having incubated them, hatched them, sheltered them from the elements and from crows, hawks, owls, gulls, and other chicknappers, and fed them tirelessly for the whole of the summer, feel under no obligation to educate them. A young eagle learns to hunt and scavenge on its own, going, in a matter of weeks, from relying on its parents to competing with them.

In early fall, there are still plenty of fish around—stripers, herrings, and alewives out in the open water, white perch, yellow perch, and carp moving with the tides across the mudflats and along the shores. Ospreys, herons, cormorants, gulls, and terns all feed upon them in their various ways. In the marshes, the rice, now ripening, is a nutritional bonanza. You can stand looking out over a marshscape and see small, dense swarms of blackbirds, bobolinks, and cowbirds at work. Out in the marsh itself are the birds you would expect to find there—herons, marsh wrens, soras, Virginia rails, bitterns, greater and lesser yellowlegs, and least, semipalmated, spotted, and solitary sandpipers —and also some you wouldn't—yellow-rumped warblers, yellowthroats, and song sparrows. In August, before they depart, I sometimes see surprising numbers of tree swallows, resting in the rice or hawking for insects just above it.

But of all the things that converge on the Bay in the late summer, ducks are by much the most vocal and obvious, and they linger longest. Their arrival gives the Bay a new character, a shot of energy and animation that is like a change of weather. And, from a predator's point of view, they represent an exceptionally abundant, exceptionally nutritious dietary supplement, even if they are not at other seasons or in other areas an important prey species to it.

I go out on the Bay in September primarily for the pleasure of watching the ducks. Once the hunting season begins, I hunt them. Several kinds of raptor at least occasionally do the same. Eagles are by far the most common of these. Apart from the eagles, and excluding ospreys, which take no interest in ducks, the raptors I see hunting around the Bay, in roughly descending order of abundance (or at least of visibility) are harriers, sharp-shins, merlins, red-tailed hawks, peregrines, goshawks, and Cooper's hawks. The number and variety of hawks are greatest in September. By mid-November, only goshawks and redtails remain. For reasons I don't understand, broad-winged hawks, quite common throughout Maine in the summer, don't seem to take an interest in the Bay per se, although I have seen as many as eighteen or twenty kettling above it, the lowest ones at twice treetop height, the highest ones, backlit by a cobalt September sky, barely visible and looking translucent, like chips of mica. Red-shouldered hawks, fairly common inland, likewise ignore the Bay, or at least elude my sight. I can recall having seen only one, and that was a long time ago. In the predawn twilight and at dusk, I see barred owls fairly often, and horned owls occasionally, and once in a while I find one or the other hunched in a tree, stoically trying to ignore a jeering paparazzi of crows. But I never see owls in the act of hunting, and don't know whether any of their depredations take place on the Bay itself, or only in the woods around it.

Peregrines—formerly known to ornithologists as duck hawks—are the only one of the Bay's raptors that is optimally equipped to hunt ducks, and they do it throughout their range. But from what I have seen, or deduced from the manner in which they hunt and/or the ways that the ducks react to them, eagles, harriers, and goshawks (and, on the rare occasion when they appear, Cooper's hawks) are willing to take advantage of the opportunity the ducks present. They are abetted by the fact that in September a few teal and mallards may still be in molt and unable to fly, and once the hunting season comes, they may find cripples—birds either entirely unable to fly, or unable to fly well enough to keep up with the flock, which makes them easy marks.

While it has been common to see raptors that are pretty clearly duck hunting around the Bay, it is surprisingly uncommon to see one actually in hot pursuit of its quarry. In my experience, it is unique, in the strictest sense of the word, to see one make a kill. The unique occasion was about twenty years ago, and I was out around the mouth of the Eastern River, which is flanked with the wide marshes known locally as the Big Flats. I noticed a hawk, soaring a few hundred feet high and maybe a quarter of a mile away. I could not identify it, and as I was trying to, it folded its tail, tilted, took a couple of fluid, deep wing beats, and went into a tuck, exactly like a downhill skier coming out of the gate. That identified it for me—a peregrine falcon, the first I'd ever seen that I could be sure of. It came down in a steep, fast diagonal, disappeared into the marsh, rose back up in a few seconds, and flew off, empty-footed. When I paddled over later, I found floating buoyantly on the surface, for all the world like the cork body of a traditional decoy, a neatly decapitated black duck. I did not know how to interpret this—a big, fine bird, cleanly killed but not eaten. I ended by interpreting it as a windfall profit, took the duck home, and ate it myself.

Harriers, much more common than peregrines, appear to be the Bay's primary raptorial duck hunter. They hunt a marsh almost exactly as a bird dog quarters a field—moving into the wind, faltering, veering, and wholly absorbed in what is immediately before them—the dog with the scents the wind brings it, the hawk with the marsh directly beneath it. The levitation of the headwind allows the hawk to hang almost motionless for a moment, then bank and tack off on an angle to it, only occasionally boosting itself along with its wings. When the time comes, it raises its wings above it and angled slightly back, and drops straight down, feet extended. It succeeds or fails out of sight. I have the impression that it succeeds fairly often. Now and again you flush a harrier as you paddle past the edge of the marsh, or up a channel through it. I have learned to get out and investigate. Once I found a hen mallard. On every other occasion when I found anything at all, it was a green-winged teal. This has occurred more often in September, before hunting season, than at any other time, and so I could be sure that the harrier hadn't simply picked off a cripple or found a duck already dead. In every case, very little remained of the duck—skeleton, feet, beak, and the outermost part of the wing. That seemed to indicate that a harrier does not abandon its prey until it is pretty well finished with it, and a good many of them may simply sit tight on their kill and let me paddle by.

For any hawk, duck hunting is all about getting within range of the duck without being seen, using some combination of stealth, speed, and concealment. For the duck, survival consists not simply of seeing the predator, but also of recognizing its species and its intentions. Harriers are among the most visible birds on the Bay—slow fliers, methodically canvassing the marsh, and seldom more than a few feet from the tips of the rice. No duck with a clear field of vision needs to fear them. The duck that needs to fear them is feeding in the rice, well hidden but with a severely limited field of vision—the patch of sky directly over its head. The duck's field of vision constitutes the harrier's window of opportunity. If the harrier enters it and sees the duck before the duck senses it overhead and dives, the odds favor the harrier. If the duck senses the harrier first, it probably escapes. From a distance, the harrier's traversing of the marsh looks casual and desultory, in the same way that a cocked mousetrap looks inert and harmless. There's a comparable kind of tensed, lethal readiness to spring and snap.

When harriers are working a marsh, I fairly often see a flock of teal rise up, fly a short distance, and resettle, sometimes right back in the place they started from. Perhaps they are simply keeping tabs. For the teal, a hawk is a specific threat in the foreground of the moment, with specific capac-

ities, methods, and limitations. Hunger, and ultimately starvation, are the constant background threats for the teal and the hawk, and they condition the behavior of each. A fat duck is able to be a lot smarter—more prudent, more circumspect, more able to feed selectively, avoiding dangerous places—than a skinny one.

The business of the harrier and the teal, like most of the other business conducted on the Bay, fluctuates with the tides. The harriers are most active when the tide is less than halfway in or more than halfway out. These are good feeding tides for ducks—they can swim among the rice stalks, picking up food off the water or tipping up and taking it off the bottom, and do so without being exposed. But this tide also presents the best opportunity for harriers and for shotgunners to get within range of them. For the shotgunner, range is about thirty-five yards; for the harrier, not much more than two or three.

If it were legal to hunt ducks with a rifle and a telescopic sight, the extremes of tide would be best. At low tide, the ducks are likely to sit in open water, or cluster on mudflats; at high tide, they may feed in the flooded rice, but are clearly visible from a great distance away. A peregrine is basically the rifleman, the telescopic sight, and the bullet, all at once. Soaring or flying, it is highly visible—like the harrier or any other predator, they've got to see their prey before it sees them. But everything changes when they tuck into their dive. This was illustrated to me this past September as I was paddling with a friend out of the Abby mouth. The tide was low, just beginning to rise, and we counted on seeing ducks later, as the water seeped up into the rice and the afternoon wore on. But suddenly we saw a single teal flying frantically and straight at us, kamikaze-style. It looked to be in full flight even as it hit the river headfirst and disappeared. And at that instant a peregrine seemed to materialize out of thin air in front of us, banking sharply away and upward, still riding the momentum of its dive. In the dive itself, coming straight at us, it had had no extension, no wing motion to attract the eye—trying to see it was about like trying to see a golf ball coming down out of the sky toward you. The peregrine's plunge, so spectacular when viewed from the side is, from the standpoint of its target, a low-profile approach, a stalk conducted at speeds that may exceed two hundred miles an hour.

Goshawks hunt from ambush, sitting in trees below the height of the forest canopy. If you are fortunate enough to see one fly across a cove and light into trees on the opposite side, it is almost impossible to locate it on its perch, even with binoculars. The bird is gray, compact, and immobile, and generally sits a few yards back in the woods, its outline broken by twigs, branches, and shadows. I have only once seen one perch in the open, on a bare snag overhanging a slough. This was at first light on a gray, foggy morning. It was very visible to me, hunkered down in my boat in a patch of marsh, because it was silhouetted against the sky. But a bird in flight would have seen—or not seen—it against a gray scrim of alders behind the snag.

They are exceptionally persistent predators. I watched one chase a dove around our house, down to the river a quarter of a mile away, and back again, before both birds disappeared over a hedgerow. It was always within a yard or two of its quarry, matching it twist for twist and turn for turn. A friend saw one crawl into a big brush pile, in pursuit of a hen. Three years ago, motoring back from a morning of hunting up the Cathance, I flushed a teal, and almost immediately a big female goshawk broke out of the woods beside the river in hot pursuit. She was directly behind the teal, but it somehow sensed her there, folded up, and plunged into the river in the same way that a kingfisher does. The hawk kept going, but I wondered if she'd have behaved differently if I hadn't been there, and perched in a tree and waited on the teal to come back to the surface, as it eventually did, and flew off in the other direction.

THESE BIRDS ALL REPAY WATCHING and invite thinking. Their activity appears to be consistently purposeful, and you can improvise at least a preliminary explanation for it, to be confirmed, complicated, or contradicted by subsequent observation. Beyond the logic of the individual hawk or species of hawk, there is the broader logic of predator and prey, their tactics and countertactics. To the extent that the prey are ducks, and you are a duck hunter, your interest may be said to be professional and pragmatic, although I would have to say, by way of parenthetical cosmic generalization, that the hard distinction between the professional and the amateur, the pragmatic and the aesthetic, is seldom as necessary as unhappy people would have you believe. Watching a harrier work a marsh is instructive. It is also a drama with a protagonist and an antagonist, bound together by the common logic of Necessity. A drama enacted on a stage, if it is good, implies the same logic, and it also guarantees, in a way that involves surprise and suspense, and yet will seem retroactively inevitable, some decisive encounter between protagonist and antagonist. The drama of the harrier and the duck offers no such guarantee. Most often, your eye follows the hawk from one end of a marsh to the other, nothing happens, and eventually the hawk wheels away and flies off to another cove. When something does happen, it only involves the hawk dropping suddenly out of your sight. The moment of its doing so is not contrived to satisfy your desire to see something enacted; it is simply something that has no reference to you, making it a good deal less than the play on the stage with respect to everything except reality.

EAGLES? WELL, AS I HAVE SAID, if you go out onto the Bay you will see them, and you won't have to sit still, look sharp, or wait long to do so. They generally perch high up in tall trees, giving them a commanding view of the Bay. And vice versa. In flight, they are unmistakable: the broad wings held horizontal, apparently as rigid as a pair of planks, when they soar, which gives them a rectilinear, cruciform aspect. Their flight from point to point is methodical, powerful, and undeviating. The breadth of their wings and the cadence of their flight come closer to that of a great blue heron or vulture than to any other raptor. When they glide just above the tree line or just below it, you have a sense of massive momentum and, if they come directly overhead, you can hear the rasp of the wind through their pinions. They are never less than impressive.

But I cannot often connect their activities to the practical business of survival. An adult male weighs eight or nine pounds. As is generally the case with raptors, the female is about 25 percent heavier—a big one can weigh as much as fourteen pounds. It is hard to calculate the food requirements of any bird—it varies with the weather, the bird's activity level, and the nutritional value of the food available to it. Raptors, like most predators, do not eat regularly— they gorge while the gorging is good, but are capable of going surprisingly long times without eating.

The best guess is that a fully fledged and self-supporting eagle needs to consume, on average, roughly a pound of food every twenty-four hours—a big female somewhat more, a small male somewhat less. A mallard a day would keep starvation away very handsomely, but it would take two teal. A fourteen-inch striper would do the job, and a big carp would be a bonanza. It would take four or five alewives, herring, or perch. Given the number of eagles on the Bay, how visible they are, and how much food is required to sustain them, you would expect them to be constantly and obviously hunting. But if they are, then it is in a strangely offhand, unfocused way.

Of other raptors around the Bay, eagles most resemble red-tailed hawks in their behavior and general proportions. Both birds spend a lot of time perched in trees, both soar easily, both are big and slow compared to falcons or goshawks, and both are versatile opportunists—generalists rather than specialists. But whether soaring or perched, a red-tail gives the impression of minutely examining the scene beneath it, circling patiently over a single pasture, or sitting in a tree—usually relatively low in it—and looking downward with the rigorous concentration of a chess player studying the board. In striking, they raise themselves quietly, unfold their wings, push off the branch, and glide downwards. They can weave their way through the understory of woods with surprising dexterity for so large a bird, ruddering with the tail, folding one wing slightly inward or downward, extending the other, never brushing against a twig or leaf. I've

never seen one go after a duck, but falconers tell me that they will kill ducks if they catch them in tight quarters—a slough or pond—and around the Bay I see them most commonly in low hardwood swamps. They appear to be primarily interested in small mammals—hares, squirrels, voles—but the bonus of a wood duck or mallard would definitely be a possibility there.

In contrast, eagles soar in a way that seems calculated to cover a lot of ground. If it is windy, they move in overlapping circles, sweeping off down the wind, wheeling back into it, hanging, and then sweeping off again. They get a fly-by view of a lot of territory this way, but do not appear to examine it very carefully. The same logic seems to apply when they perch—they can see far and wide, but appear to scan the scene in front of them the way a lookout on a ship would, not looking for some small inconspicuous thing close at hand, but for some big, distant thing. The red-tail behaves like a bird that hopes to capture an alert, elusive creature by stealth and speed; the eagle behaves like a bird that expects something big and hapless to show up, not to be captured so much as to be appropriated.

They do show a good deal of interest in ducks, and I sometimes see an eagle gliding over the rice below treetop level, rather in the manner of a harrier, although generally when the tide is higher. In the process of doing this, they may swerve downward enough to flush a flock of teal, but they don't pursue it, and I assume they are simply checking to see if one of the little ducks is in any way impaired and vulnerable. In terms of its length and wingspan, an eagle is twice the size of a harrier, but it weighs ten times as much. In terms of aerial buoyancy, hang time, and maneuverability, they are to the harrier as a paper airplane is to a kite.

Twice, in the October just past, I watched a juvenile eagle—probably the same one—dealing with a crippled duck. The first time I was hunting over decoys. The eagle, coming low over the marsh, abruptly banked and circled back, with a mighty flailing of wings. It continued to circle as tightly as it could, several times hovering just above the water and reaching downward with its talons, as though to seize the duck. The tide was nearly high, but there was enough vegetation to screen the duck itself from my view. It would apparently dive at the last moment, forcing the eagle to rise up and circle back. It looked like a 747 trying to land on an aircraft carrier—just too big and too clumsy for the job. Finally—something I had never seen before—it actually set itself down in the water, holding its wings high above it, and apparently groped downward for the submerged duck. That could not possibly succeed—there was a good four feet of water beneath it. After a minute or so, it gave up, lifted off, and flew up into some pines behind me.

It was near quitting time, and I'd seen no ducks flying for the past hour or so. I considered paddling out, finding the cripple, and shooting it before it could dive. A duck is a duck is a feast, and I would, in addition, be saving this one from a slower but no less certain death. I and my kind, and not the eagle, were now the alpha predators, able to expropriate the prey of other predators. But it struck me that I did not hunt in order to exercise dominion over the fowls of the air and the beasts of the field so much as to enter the calculus of their existence. There was the young eagle; there were snapping turtles, raccoons, foxes, owls, and gulls—plenty of resourceful carnivores lurking in and around and above the Bay, gleaning the tide flats. The duck would not be wasted.

Two weeks later, I was hunting with Arthur Middleton, a friend who is also a falconer and who'd spent the summer in charge of an eagle-restoration project in downstate New York. He'd assumed responsibility for four eagle chicks—imports from Wisconsin—in May. They were placed in a hack box—a sort of enclosed tree house, high above the ground—and every day he'd climbed a long ladder up to this artificial aerie to feed and check them over. When they were fledged, he opened the box and let them out into the tree, where they could learn to clamber, hop, and eventually to fly. All four, having been equipped with high-tech tracking devices, were now making their way in the world—he'd just heard from one that, with a fine youthful disregard for conventional wisdom, had flown straight north, and was now disporting itself in Quebec. Another, apparently interested in a different kind of tourism, was hanging around the Antietam battlefield, down in Maryland.

After a morning of more hunting than shooting, and more shooting than slaying, we were motoring out of the Androscoggin mouth on the Topsham side, along the edge of what is known as Windmill Cove, for a reason no longer obvious. As we approached the end of Pleasant Point, we saw an adult eagle, circling just over the rice—surely after a cripple, we thought. But a little further on, we saw a movement of big dark wings in the marsh ahead of us—a juvenile eagle, or *the* juvenile eagle, again sitting on the water, holding its wings high, and apparently reaching down with its feet. I shut off the motor. The eagle, fifty yards away, took no notice of us. It was a very strange sight. The bird was not using its wings, simply holding them aloft, in the manner of a ballerina pirouetting on tiptoe, or the Winged Victory of Samothrace. Later, Arthur told me that an eagle's wings (as opposed, for example, to those of an osprey) are so broad and big that if they get thoroughly wet the eagle cannot lift them off the water, and must use them in a rowing, butterfly-stroke fashion to propel itself to shore and shake them dry. This one, like the one a fortnight earlier, finally gave up and took off. It was carrying the rootball of a clump of rice, with the long stems of the rice trailing out behind—perhaps the stems had tangled in its talons, or it had clutched them, felt the resistance of the root, and imagined that it had seized its prey.

I turned to restart the motor, and as I did so the adult eagle, which we'd lost track of, suddenly appeared, gliding rapidly with its talons half-lowered, almost touching the water. When it reached the spot where the young bird had been, it canted its body slightly upward and thrust its legs straight down, hardly interrupting its forward progress, and kept on going, but now with a duck—it looked to be either a black or a hen mallard—in its clutches. That, at least, was a clear instance of predatory guile and skill. It had come in low, without flapping, partially screened from the duck by the marsh. The duck, no doubt exhausted and seeming to have escaped, could not get itself back underwater fast enough or deep enough this time.

I asked Arthur if perhaps this was a case of a parent bird collaborating with its offspring, showing it the ropes in the process. He thought not. He pointed out to me—I wouldn't have noticed otherwise—that the young bird was almost certainly a female, and the mature one a male. She was substantially bigger than he. And Arthur said that juvenile birds were especially likely to drive mature ones, including their own parents, away from a kill—dependency prolonging itself as aggression, a not entirely unfamiliar behavior among adolescents of another feather.

Twice—each time in November—I've seen something that surprised me—an eagle appearing over a cove where a

Waiting out the winter

big gang of black ducks and mallards were feeding, and every duck in the cove going airborne in an instant, with much alarmed quacking, and heading for the horizon. The first time was when I was new to Maine, to the Bay, and to its eagles, and I noticed and remembered it only because one of the ducks that had flushed—a black—had passed over my head, and I'd killed it. I had never again seen ducks get particularly agitated by the proximity of eagles. I had seen teal and big duck feeding just under a headland with big pines on it, where eagles regularly perched, and several times had watched two or three eagles sitting on a sandbar, while in a small tidal lagoon behind it several hundred ducks gabbled and dabbled contentedly. But then last year I'd had a repeat of the earlier experience. I was sculling in toward Center Cove when a big flock of mostly black ducks passed over me, set their wings, circled, and pitched into the cove. I slowed down, to give them time to disperse and begin feeding, which might improve my chances of sculling within range of one. An eagle—a second-year bird by the look of it—came over very much as the ducks had done, headed for the cove, and as it did there was a great kerfluffle and clamor of wings, and every duck in it left with an urgency suggesting serious consternation, if not outright panic.

I'd pulled in the oar, stoppered the oar port, and was putting the motor on the transom when I heard another boat approaching, looked up, and saw John Edgecomb in his big gunning float. I waited on him to come up—I seem to learn something every time I talk to him. He pulled alongside, shut off his motor, and asked if I was going to put decoys in the cove. I said not, and told him about the eagle.

"Happens every time," he said.

I said something to the effect that I'd almost never seen ducks get so exercised by the mere appearance of an eagle.

"All according to the tide. There's about a foot of water over the flats right now, and no grass to speak of. An eagle can reach down a foot, foot and a half, easy—those legs are longer than you think. Diving's how a duck gets away from any danger that's already up in the air over it. And diving wouldn't have done these ducks any good at all."

We went our ways—he to set out his decoys in the cove, I to go investigate the Muddy River. As I motored in that direction, I thought to myself that what he'd said made perfect sense, but that I'd have never put two and two together that way and understood that the ducks' jumpiness was inversely proportioned to the depth of the water. When you hunt, you think of flight as being a duck's only evasive tactic and exit strategy. But it's clearly not when an eagle is the hunter.

I have taken to asking hunters I know—men who, like John Edgecomb, began hunting on the Bay with their fathers, and never stopped—if they'd ever seen an eagle kill a duck that wasn't already crippled. Only John had—he saw one come in low over the trees and swoop down on a single black duck in a cove. He said it happened in a hurry, and the duck seemed entirely unaware of the eagle until it was much too late. But everybody had seen big gangs of ducks flush from a cove or from the open, sandy shallows in the Androscoggin mouth when an eagle hove into view, and they agreed that, when geese had been more common on the Bay, they were exceptionally aware of eagles, and would get restive and uneasy when one appeared even at a great distance.

But Ronnie Burrell had seen something remarkable. He had been standing on Center Point, looking out across the Abby marshes towards Browns Point and the Kennebec, and he saw a swan, in itself almost a once-in-a-lifetime bird around the Bay, flying northward up the Kennebec. As it approached Brown's Point, it lifted up, evidently in order to fly over rather than under the big transmission lines there. As it did so, an eagle—"I never seen him, and I don't think that swan ever saw him either. He must have been soaring way the hell up"—came out of nowhere and hit the swan from above. "That swan looked like he been shot—wobbling and thrashing and coming down. But he got away, as well as I could tell. The eagle pulled up and flew on off. Maybe the swan dived or got into the trees somehow—I couldn't be sure from where I was."

WHEREVER THEY OCCUR, eagles have been birds of omen, associated in myth and legend with forces of awesome power—the sun, thunder, and lightning, emperors, monarchs, armies. John James Audubon, whose paintings so often hover between science and mythology, saw eagles hunting swans in the fall of 1820 as he drifted down the Mississippi on a flatboat, paying for his passage by killing enough game to feed the crew, and drawing and painting birds in his spare time. He described how pairs of eagles hunted from perches and usually in tandem, waiting for a solitary swan to appear:

> As the Swan is passing the dreaded pair, starts from his perch, in full preparation for the chase, the male bird, with an awful scream, that to the Swan's ear brings more terror than the report of a large duck-gun. Now is the moment to witness the display of the Eagle's powers. He glides through the air like a falling star, and, like a flash of lightning, comes upon the timorous quarry, which now, in agony and despair, seeks by various maneuvers to elude the grasp of his cruel talons. It mounts, doubles, and would willingly plunge into the stream, were it not prevented by the Eagle....

The eagle eventually drives the swan toward shore, strikes it, brings it to earth, and delivers the *coup de grâce*:

> [The eagle] presses down with his powerful feet, and drives his sharp claws deeper into the heart of the dying Swan. He shrieks with delight, as he feels the last convulsions of his prey, which has now sunk under his unceasing efforts to render death as painfully felt as it can possibly be.

Audubon insisted that, as a writer and a painter, he was first and foremost an ornithologist, but what we have here suggests that his observations of the eagle were, in fact, influenced by its mythic associations with tyrants and vengeful gods, and with dangerous or portentous heavenly disturbances. His painting of the bald eagle, triumphing over a slain catfish against a backdrop of rugged peaks and stormy skies, is so powerful that it overcomes one's practical objections—for example, that catfish do not occur in mountainous terrain. The wonderful immediacy of his rendering of the bird itself makes such caveats seem ridiculous. But his prose, in this passage and elsewhere, is fairly dreadful, and one feels no compunction in pointing out that eagles neither shriek nor scream—their most assertive and aggressive vocalization is a feeble, high-pitched, parched noise, halfway between cackling and chirping.

Audubon's description of the eagle and the swan uses a rhetorical, conventional, and inflated rhetoric to try to convey the experience of sublimity—an aesthetic experience in

The way of an eagle in the air

which our pleasure is not separable from terror and revulsion. His gifts as a writer were not equal to the occasion. But I think that, in visualizing the scene—not simply the eagle and the swan, but also the huge, unconstricted river, with the staggering numbers and varieties of birds moving down it— we can easily imagine that it was in fact sublime—awe-inspiring, compelling, and frightening. The human presence on the river was puny and technologically rudimentary—flatboats, keel boats, rafts, and canoes, set against the vast expanse of water and swamp, and the passionate, headlong, and implacable energies of Nature, as epitomized by the two enormous birds.

What Ronnie saw, roughly a century and a half later, has a different resonance. Eagle and swan are now framed by the transmission lines and the two towering pylons that carry them across the river. These things are reminders of the human domination, which now appears irreversible, of the landscape and everything it contains. The fearsome energy of electricity—the flash of lightning that Audubon equated to the attacking eagle—has been domesticated, regulated, and turned into a commodity. The swan and eagle encountering each other over Brown's Point seem almost like one of those re-enactments of a Civil War battle. The world they evoke is remote from us. Because it poses no threat or challenge, we can view it nostalgically, projecting our own imaginative longings onto it. It is not that the eagle and the swan over

Brown's Point were any less authentic than the ones that Audubon saw. It is that our relation to them and to the world of natural violence and wildness that they epitomize is now selective and recreational, rather than involuntary and essential. The sense of the supernatural no longer lurks within the natural; the eagle seems less like an agent of unpredictable and terrible gods than like a cultural artifact— our national bird; the protagonist of one of the environmental movement's most heartening success stories; a barometer of ecological recovery.

That eagles are pervasive around the Bay is a good omen, even if it guarantees nothing. On the day after Arthur Middleton and I watched the adult bird, the juvenile, and the crippled duck, we hunted again, this time well up the Androscoggin, and we'd had a moderately successful, or at least not wholly unsuccessful, morning of it. At midday, we decided to put out decoys off the foot of Cow Island and eat lunch there. As we did so, we were able to watch two adult eagles across the river from us. They were at work on a new nest. It was at this point about the size of a crow's nest, and still very flimsy looking. The birds were bringing surprisingly long sticks—usually the outer end of a rotten branch, branchlets, twigs, and all, and between three and four feet long—up into the big pine where the nest was located. We were not positioned so that we could see how they placed the new stick onto the nest—whether or not they broke it in two, or made any effort to set it solidly in place, or simply added it to the rubbishy accumulation of material that was already there. Once, we saw the female fly just over a dead tree on Cow Island, swipe down with her feet, and snap off a four-foot branch, scarcely breaking the rhythm of her flight to do so.

Their nest was in full sight of Route 1, a very busy stretch of road. From it, the town of Brunswick, the Sea Dog Pub, and two major bridges across the Androscoggin would be clearly visible. Arthur said it was surprising for eagles to build in such close proximity to human activity. In general, they want exactly the kind of site that every realtor in Maine also wants—shoreline frontage, lots of privacy, extensive water views. That a pair of eagles were willing to commit themselves to a suboptimal location might be taken as an indication that the Bay itself was a sufficiently desirable neighborhood for the eagles to overcome their normal agoraphobia in order to claim a place on it. We found that a cheering speculation as we ate our lunch, chatted, and watched the tide come in. Then we got back to hunting, and continued until quitting time, ending the day with another couple of ducks, and a fine, self-exonerating sense of weariness and accomplishment.

I kept thinking back to that pair of eagles and their nest—the first time I had seen eagles actually building. That led to a much older memory, of the first eagles' nest I had ever seen, in Maine or anywhere else. It was about three decades ago, and we'd gone with our children and some friends and their children to camp overnight on Swan Island. Late in the afternoon, a warden stopped by the campground to be certain we were in the right place, chatted for a while, and offered to take us on a brief tour of the island. We climbed onto the back of a big flatbed truck and he drove us down the sandy road that runs along the spine of the island, and then he stopped in front of an abandoned house. The house itself would have been worth stopping for—it looked to be early nineteenth century, the kind of place that, when you are young, you dream of finding and fixing up. But now it was past repair—the rooftree sagging from the gable ends down toward the central chimney, the shingles mangy with lichen and moss, the sill collapsing under the front door.

Behind the house was an old, spreading hardwood—an oak. It was long since dead. And in it, perhaps the cause of its demise, was the eagles' nest. The warden said it was the biggest one in the state, which was easy to believe. He guesstimated its weight at better than a ton. It looked like an inverted beaver lodge—just a big heap of sticks that had built up over the years, and now had a cubic footage that would equal that of a subcompact car—a VW Beetle, say. Eagles had at that time almost entirely stopped nesting on the Bay—the warden told us that from Richmond all the way down to the mouth of the Kennebec, there were dozens of nests, but no more than one or two of them would be active in any given year. And even those one or two seldom produced chicks that lived long enough to fly away from them.

It was, now that I thought about it all these years later, an odd place for an eagles' nest—it had at least that in common with the one Arthur and I had seen. To begin with, it was much lower than usual, and much further from the water. At the time we saw it, the Bay would not have been visible from it, although it might have been when the nest was first constructed, before the deserted island had grown back up in pine, hemlock, and oak. Surely the eagles had not begun building it until the house was abandoned, which could have been no later than 1936, but might have been quite a lot earlier. The warden didn't know how long the nest had been active, or how many years had passed since eagles last used it. Like the house, it made you think of generations that had established something and stuck with it, but had in time succumbed to changes in the world beyond them. Had there been a day when someone who had grown up in that house had come back, just to look at it and remember the past, and found the eagles building there? That would have been a melancholy, chilling sight on the now empty island, with its other boarded, shuttered, and untenanted houses, like something out of the antiquity of an older civilization:

They say the Lion and the Lizard keep
The Courts where Jamshyd gloried and drank deep;
And Bhram, that great Hunter—the Wild Ass
Stamps o'er his head, but cannot break his sleep.

Now even the wild creatures that had taken possession of the backyard tree were gone, and it seemed at the time that their whole species might in its turn be on the way to oblivion.

And yet now the eagles are back, although with a changed meaning. We once took them as they have traditionally been taken—as emblems of a proud invincibility. Now, whenever we see them, they are reminders, first and foremost, of our belated efforts on their behalf—efforts that were a symptom of a nation's prosperity, confidence, and generosity, and its desire to begin to make amends. They have become the symbol of our better nature, and the extent to which we believe in it.

It remains to be seen whether the pair building on the Androscoggin will carry the task through to its conclusion, nest and raise their young there. From what I read, eagles sometimes seem to build nests on spec, perhaps as a mere exercise in pair-bonding; in those cases, they never complete and actually use the nest. I hoped that these two were in earnest. Some years ago, the town of Brunswick built a fine pathway for pedestrians and cyclists to use in the narrow strip of land between Route One and the river. It is used faithfully by all sorts of people; I have sometimes used it myself, just for the civilized pleasure of the thing. It would be nice if next summer those walkers and bikers and joggers and roller-bladers could look up and see the eagles in their comings and goings, and eventually see the fully fledged young bird taking its first flights and learning its trade.

Nothing beats that kind of education, and people who come to feel they have an emotional stake in seeing those big birds may also come to recognize that they have an emotional stake in the Bay and the river, about which we know so little of what there is to know.

Guzzle and grass, mallards and teal

The Wild Crop

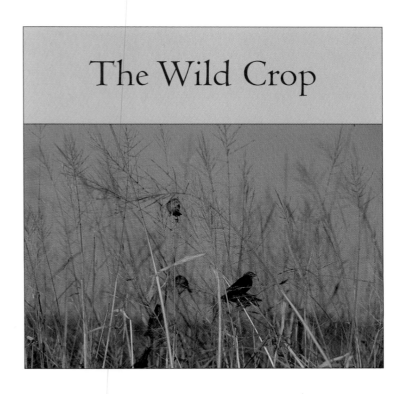

EUROPEANS FIRST ENCOUNTERED grasses of the *Zizania* genus in the New World, and did not immediately agree about what to call them. In the vicinity of the Great Lakes, the French trappers, explorers, and missionaries referred to the species growing there as *folle avoine*—wild oats. English colonists along the Atlantic seaboard had the same idea, and at first called the plant water or marsh oat. The northerly habitat of the plant, its pale green color, tasseled head, long stalk, and narrow-bladed leaves were no doubt responsible for this identification. A stand of it might easily be mistaken for a field of oats, were it not for the great disparity in size and, upon closer examination, the pronounced dissimilarity of the seeds of the two plants.

The other name given to the plant was suggested by the fact that it grew in water, and especially by the shape and texture of the grain: wild, Canadian, or Indian rice. The resemblance of its grain to that of the true rices held good in the kitchen and at the table, where early Euro-Americans found it a very satisfactory substitute for cultivated rice.

Strictly speaking, oats, domestic rice, wheat, barley, rye, and corn belong, like wild rice, to the world's great family of grasses, and all of them existed as wild plants long before they were domesticated. As a general proposition, the domestic form of a plant tends to replace the wild one entirely, or to reduce its range very drastically, usually to remote areas where agriculture is impossible. Around the Bay, wild rice flourishes without benefit of agronomy and its life cycle differs significantly from that of any domesticated grain.

THE NATURAL WORLD IS OBSESSIVELY CONCERNED with investment strategies. And, as celebrated CEOs remind us, by being either hugely successful or indicted, timing is everything in investment—you've got to know when to buy and when to sell, when to scam, and when to scram. The strategy of wild rice is predicated on the fact that its circumstances are liquid but its assets are not. It grows in water but has no offshore accounts; it must raise its own seed money, which is the only kind of money it has. Its treasury is a tempting target for fly-by-night profit takers, against which duck hunters provide, at best, a very limited kind of protection. It keeps on investing entirely in itself, plowing all of its assets into its redevelopment budget, which is also its pension fund. The whole enterprise goes belly up every autumn and starts from scratch the following spring. If it were a business instead of an aquatic plant, it would be a professional baseball team, with the home office, perhaps, on Yawkey Way, appropriately proximate to the Boston fens.

To speak more plainly, wild rice is an annual. On the Bay, long mats of dead and sodden stems are drifting back and forth on every tide by mid-November, and if you walk along the beach at Popham, where the Kennebec empties into the sea, you find windrows of them as flotsam along the dune line. The seeds that are not eaten by bobolinks, blackbirds, cowbirds, sparrows, soras, ducks, geese, and caterpillars and have not been carried by the current into water that is too deep or washed high and dry by wave action, settle into the mud of the tide flats and spend the winter there. They are programmed not to germinate until they have spent at least three months under ooze and water that gets no warmer than thirty-five degrees. Once that dormancy is over, they will germinate when the water temperature climbs back up to about forty-five degrees. The roots form first, then shoots, or tillers, grow up from them. There may be as few as three or four tillers per root, or as many as fifty, depending on how closely the roots are spaced. They grow rapidly through the summer and are full-grown by Labor Day. Even when the plant is full-grown, and higher than your head, the root system is surprisingly small, and can be pulled out of the muck with less effort than it takes to pull a carrot from the finest and least compacted soil.

A group of old guides and hunters used to have an annual late-summer competition to see who could bring in the tallest stalk of wild rice. The all-time record was something over thirteen feet. An average height seems to me rather hard to arrive at. In the best marshes, particularly the one that runs parallel to the Kennebec channel at the mouth of the Abby, the height would be eight or ten feet; but in other marshes, even when the crop is good, the plants are a foot or more shorter. They are shorter yet in the upper reaches of the Abby, Cathance, Muddy, and Eastern Rivers. I do not know if there is a correlation between the height of the rice and the tidal range of the particular marsh or not. Even the shortest rice on the Bay is much taller than the rice I see growing inland, on lakes and streams, where it seems to average about three feet.

John Lichter, in the Department of Environmental Studies at Bowdoin, says that it is unusual for an annual to dominate a vegetative community so completely as wild rice dominates the Bay. Usually, woody species or species that regenerate from the root would be expected to crowd out annuals, because they have such a great competitive advantage in the spring and early summer. In looking at the Bay and thinking about it, John speculates that ice may play a crucial role. At low tide it rests directly on the mud, and is lifted off at high tide. It would tend to crush, grind, and otherwise eradicate perennial roots and branches. The rice seed may be moved around when the ice shifts, particularly in the spring as it begins to break up, but it is not damaged.

John also finds that the seed production is very high—

the plant has the classic strategy of any species that is at the bottom of the food chain. An endemic worm in some years becomes more or less epidemic, and every tasseled head (properly called the inflorescence) of every stalk seems to have been invaded. But even then, the rice manages to deposit enough grain to hold ducks in their normal numbers until late in the fall, and to regenerate itself the following spring.

Z. aquatica—the predominant species in the Bay—seems never to have been relied upon by human beings as a significant source of nourishment, and there is no evidence that either the Bay's indigenous peoples or the early Europeans paid much attention to it. *Z. palustris*, the predominant species in the Great Lakes Basin, is a very different story, having been an important dietary staple there for at least two millennia. The Ojibwa, whom the Europeans first found in the vicinity of Lake Huron, and who drifted from there westward to Minnesota and beyond, relied on it as the staff of life, and attached a religious importance to the rituals of its harvesting and preparation. The wild rice that we buy in stores is of this species, and most of it comes from Minnesota and Wisconsin. By far the greater portion of it is now domesticated, sowed and grown in flooded fields, and harvested mechanically.

When a wild plant is domesticated, its investment strategy is modified. For human purposes, there are two inconvenient things about the strategy that wild rice has evolved.

The first is that the crop does not mature all at the same time. Some seeds are ripe and ready for harvest early in September; others will not be until a month or six weeks later. This is true even of the seeds on a single tiller. The logic of this seems pretty clear. At any specific time, the seeds might be vulnerable to conditions of exceptionally high or low water, to an early freeze-up, or to huge concentrations of seed-eating insects or migratory birds. So the plant creates the botanical equivalent of a balanced portfolio, timing its investment so that losses at one season can be offset by gains at another.

From a human standpoint, the second disadvantage of wild rice is that it "shatters" easily. "Shatter" in this sense refers to the dispersing of the seeds from the stalk. In the case of wild rice, the ripe seed falls with only the slightest disturbance of the stalk, which would leave a human harvester, unless he were very careful and very skilled, with only unripe seeds to harvest. The Ojibwa got around this by using canoes. The paddler moved the boat ahead in a straight line; the harvester had two sticks, each about a yard long. With one of these, she reached out with her right hand and bent a clump of rice carefully over the boat, then beat the stalks gently with the stick in her left hand. Then she reached out to the other side, now using the left hand to gather and the right hand to thresh. The canoe glided ahead as she did this. By all accounts it was a delicate art, not easily mastered. Bend the stalks over the canoe too roughly, and your harvest falls into the water. Thresh them too heartily, and you get a lot of inedible green grain mixed in with the harvest.

In turning Z. palustris into a cultivated plant, agronomists have worked to make the grain more shatterproof and to produce a greater uniformity of maturation. The extent of their success is indicated by the fact that wild rice is common and affordable in our supermarkets. But it is not entirely wild—its investment strategy is now guided by an alien philosophy.

As an annual, wild rice is like any other crop, having some years that are better and some that are worse. The current year has seemed exceptionally poor to those of us who take an interest in such things; two years ago, in 2003, it was exceptionally good. Old-timers are generally of the view that such fluctuations are common, but also of the view that, while the marshes have not diminished in acreage in the last half century, they are, even in their best years, less dense than in the past. The biggest change to the Bay during that period has been the cleaning up of the Androscoggin and Kennebec, and they speculate that the rice may have been to some extent fertilized by the unholy and unwholesome amalgam of organic and chemical effluent that poured into it.

Except for John Lichter and his students, those of us who take an interest in the rice crop in the Bay are duck hunters. Insofar as we are concerned, the plant is the staff of

The foot of Swan Island, high tide

life, and a leading indicator of what kind of season we have coming. In the late summer of a good year, when the stands of it are tall and dense, there is a serious kind of satisfaction merely in looking at it, as though you were a farmer surveying his acres. The tassels are in various stages of blossom and fruition. The blossoms themselves are hardly worthy of the name, only a few pale and flimsy petals, not much bigger than a hemlock needle, and the grain develops inconspicuously, little sheathed swellings of the tassels. If you pick an unripe one and peel it, you find a pith of starchy white. When fully ripe, the grains are a mahogany brown, perhaps somewhat thinner than their semi-domesticated cousins on the supermarket shelves, but otherwise identical to them.

Heavy wind and hard cold lay the marshes low, but not all marshes at the same time. Some—for example, the ones at the mouth of the Eastern River—are generally falling before September is over; others remain upright until the end of October, although considerably thinned out. It is analogous to the shedding of leaves in a deciduous woods: a new sense of sparseness and an intimation of the cold desolation that is to come. But by this point, the rice has done its work, seeding the flats abundantly. In all but the poorest years, the ducks will continue to find rice enough to hold them on the Bay until the shallows begin to freeze, and things go dormant for another year.

W HEN THE LAST ICE IS FINALLY GONE from the Bay, and May is in the offing, the first vegetation—a scattered, unpromising stubble—pokes up through the mud. By the end of the month, it appears from a distance like a thin, green haze when the tide is low, but it grows steadily through the summer. By midsummer, when the upland grasses are beginning to lose their verdure and look a bit weary, the Bay, immune to drought, is coming into its most beautiful season. The rice still has that tender greenness of early spring, but is now as high as a man's head, and if you paddle close beside it you get a distinctively vegetative smell, something like the smell of humus and not at all like the thick pungency of a salt marsh. Bobolinks are among the first migrants to visit it, and among the first to leave. By mid-August, blue-winged teal have begun to show up; at high tide you can watch them, dainty little ducks swimming among the tips of the rice, feeding on the heads that are heaviest with grain, which droop conveniently down to within their reach. The blue-wings will depart early—most have left before the hunting begins, early in October; the green-wings, blacks, and mallards will succeed them, and find that the crop is still ripe and ripening for the picking—the harvest, and then the gleaning, go on and on, from the measured bounty of this lanky, unlikely grass.

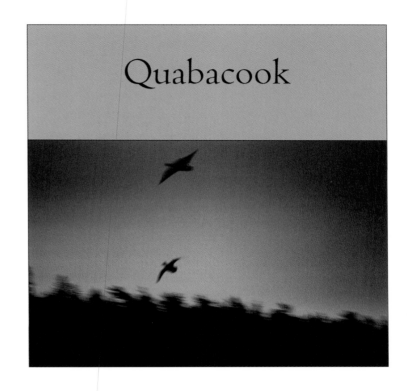

Quabacook

THERE'S NO AGREEMENT AS TO WHY the first English settlers called the Bay Merrymeeting. In the context of seventeenth-century English and New English culture, *merry* was not just another adjective. It rankled Puritans, who associated it with celebrations like Christmas, which they deemed to be a nominally Christian but essentially pagan and ungodly feast, one with all sorts of convivial whoop-de-doo and cheerful carnality. Anglicans naturally liked the word, if only because it so scandalized and aggravated a group of people whom they considered self-righteous kill-joys of the deadliest sort. In Massachusetts, the defiantly impious Thomas Morton set up a community of jolly souls who wanted nothing to do with John Winthrop, the City on a Hill, and all of that, and named it Merry Mount. It didn't last long; he was driven back to England, and it became Quincy.

In the context of that time, a *merrymeeting* was a festive gathering—generally, it would seem, an impromptu one, where a lot of spontaneous merrymaking took place. It has been speculated that the name refers chiefly to the seasonal movements of the Abenaki—the Bay was a place of rendevous for the tribes from the Androscoggin and Kennebec watersheds. That doesn't seem especially likely to me—their own name for the Bay had no such reference. It might more plausibly have come from the springtime reunions of trappers and traders, native Americans and Euro-Americans, which would presumably have been as convivial as cheap rum and brandy could make them. But my guess is that the name had more to do with the English culture wars than with local events, and that it was intended to appeal to one kind of English colonist and warn off another. The fact that one cove downriver from the Bay is named *Robinhood* and another *Christmas* tends to support this: both names, to a Puritan, would have smacked of Merry Olde England, which was precisely the anathema they were fleeing.

In any event, the name colonized and familiarized the place, at least for some Englishmen, and it comes trippingly off the tongue, the smoothly alliterative and trochaically upbeat adjective followed by the more sombrely nautical and curtly expansive *bay*. Leaving all that warfare over vocabulary, ecclesiastical governance, predestination, and the rest of it aside, it is one of the better English placenames in the New World. But some of us might prefer the name it replaced.

THE ABENAKI KNEW MERRYMEETING BAY as *Quabacook*. The word means "duck watering place." The first syllable practically quacks, all by itself. So even back at the time when the Bay swarmed with anadromous fish and eagles congregated around it like seagulls around a garbage dump, its great, defining feature was its status as a habitat for waterfowl. It meant ducks.

That remains the case today—to the extent that the Bay is known beyond the towns that immediately border it, and to the extent that it is identified with anything, it is as a place of ducks and duck hunting. And of the various livelihoods, subcultures, and distinctive traditions that have flourished around Quabacook over the course of its long history, the one that unselfconsciously continues is the one of duck hunting.

The chapters that follow are going to be about that— about ducks and duck hunting—both because of their continuing importance to the Bay, and because such direct and indirect knowledge and experience of the Bay as I have comes far more from hunting than from anything else. A good many people feel an innate aversion to hunting, and I promise not to try to argue anybody out of it. In turn, I hope that those people will not boycott this section of the book, or feel that they cannot read it without implicitly condoning something which they believe to be wrong. One may, after all, read a murder mystery or a military history without condoning retail or wholesale homicide.

Hunter Education

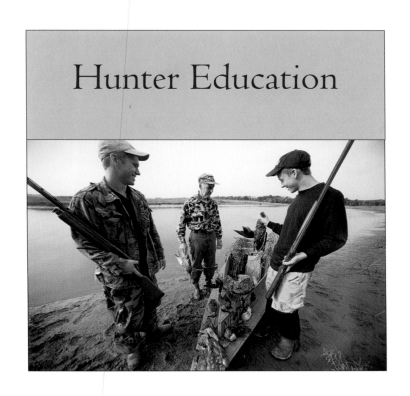

L ET'S START WITH THOREAU. The eleventh chapter of
Walden is called "Higher Laws." In it, you would expect to
find Thoreau the transcendentalist, Thoreau the student of
Oriental, Greco-Roman, and Judaeo-Christian religious traditions, and eventually you do. But the chapter opens like
this:

> As I came home through the woods with my string of
> fish, trailing my pole, it being now quite dark, I caught a
> glimpse of a woodchuck stealing across my path, and felt
> a strange thrill of savage delight, and was strongly
> tempted to seize and devour him raw; not that I was
> hungry then, except for that wildness which he repre-
> sented.

He goes on to talk about hunting and fishing, to which he
attributes his own early and passionate attachment to Nature.
He acknowledges that he had some years previously put aside
his gun, because he preferred live birds to dead ones. But
notwithstanding his eventual renunciation of the sport,

> I am compelled to doubt if any equally valuable sports

are ever substituted for it; and when some of my friends have asked me anxiously about their boys, whether they should let them hunt, I have answered yes—remembering that it was one of the best parts of my education;—*make* them hunters, though only sportsmen at first, if possible mighty hunters at last, so that they shall not find game large enough for them in this or any vegetable wilderness,—hunters as well as fishers of men. Thus far I am of the opinion of Chaucer's [monk], who

> yave not of that text a pulled hen
> That saith that hunters ben not holy men.

Thoreau was no early apologist for the NRA. He goes on to make it clear that the boy should ideally progress from the hunter to the naturalist/philosopher, as he himself had done. But, speaking both for himself and in general, he considered hunting a crucial evolutionary state, for the individual as well as the species. Even men who never outgrow it are introduced by it to the woods, the waters, and to what he calls "the most original parts of themselves."

Geographically, historically, culturally, and so forth, my own childhood stood at a great distance from Thoreau's. Its intellectual resources were fewer, its literacy was shallower, and its recognition of an inward and spiritual life was less confident, and therefore less nurtured and

attended to. But I can echo his statement with absolute certainty—hunting was one of the best parts of my education. I have sometimes felt ashamed for having never outgrown it, but I have never for an instant regretted my early exposure to it, or that I spent so few of my elementary and secondary school days acquiring much in the way of social or athletic proficiency, and so many of them hunting and fishing, or dreaming or thinking or talking or reading about hunting and fishing.

My circumstances did resemble Thoreau's in that I not only hunted and fished, I grew up in a time and place where a great many men and boys did so, with varying degrees of passion and fidelity. I was ten years old before my father took me to a pond and we hunkered together in a blind—me with a borrowed .410 shotgun—and I really and truly hunted. But already by then a great deal of my playing, whether alone or with friends, had pointed in that direction—a sort of make-believe hunting carried on in backyards and vacant lots. It was a matter of flushing meadowlarks out of a patch of broom straw and pretending that they were quail, or pretending that the juncos that scratched around the edge of the yard were a flock of pintails or summer duck. The pleasure of it was the pleasure of that most basic childhood game, the one of hiding and seeking. I could lie utterly still under Mama's big forsythia bush and have the juncos feed to within an arm's length of me, and that was something special, a breathless interruption of my ordinary sense of who I was and almost of what species I belonged to.

I wasn't then and am not now a naturalist, in any even moderately serious sense of the word. But by the time I was taken on that first hunting trip, I could identify the fish, amphibians, reptiles, mammals, and birds that were at all common in my immediate world. This knowledge was neither encouraged nor discouraged by grownups—it was an accidental by-product of solitude, fantasy, and game playing that all began with stepping outdoors. And an attentiveness to critters led to an attentiveness to landscapes, of a sort that was still rooted in the hide-and-seek impulse. Every brush pile or rotting log could hide or harbor something. Roll over the log, and nine times out of ten you'd find only the usual centipedes, grubs, beetles, and the oversized, pale earthworms that were called spankers and were too brittle for bait. But on the tenth time, there would be a newt, or a big, flat-headed and villainous-looking skink, or the odd, limbless lizard known as a glass snake, because of the ease with which it parted from its tail if you tried to pick it up that way. These were discoveries, buried treasures of a sort. Their allure was enhanced by their dank, moldering, crypt- or tomb-like lurking places.

This fascination with critters does not happen only to children raised within the culture of hunting. It is observable in a great many children, to say nothing of kittens and pup-
pies, and may have to do with what E. O. Wilson calls "biophilia"—"our innate tendency to focus on life and lifelike processes." But hunting, at least in the time, place, and manner in which I came to it, deepened and confirmed the craving. It was still hiding and seeking, but now in a way that was entirely earnest, and took me beyond the backyards and ditch banks and vacant lots, and into the adjacent and bigger worlds of farms and fields, woods, swamps, ponds, rivers, and salt marshes.

THERE ARE OTHER THINGS ABOUT HUNTING, some of them counterintuitive, if your intuitions have not been shaped by it. I believe all serious hunters develop some sense of the sanctity of their quarry. This is not to be confused with a mere respect for the animal's wariness, toughness, and so forth—it is a good deal less rational and more powerful than that. The landscapes and seasons in which you hunt belong to the animal; it is their soul, the thing that makes them alive. Your encounters with the animal are memorable, not to be taken lightly. Historians of myth speak of the strange affinity between violence and the sacred, and it is possible to rationalize this in biophilic terms—our piety toward life naturally involving a sacrifice of it, and vice versa. But this is getting rather fancy and far afield. Thoreau gives us a simple proposition: "Perhaps the hunter is the greatest friend of the animals hunted, not excepting the Humane

Society." The whole structure of his chapter on "Higher Laws" rests on the assumption that our religious impulse—our capacity for reverence—originates somewhere in the neighborhood of our predatory one.

So THAT WAS ONE KIND OF EDUCATION. In college, I got seriously involved with other kinds of education, especially literary education. Such education often has (often *must* have) a disorienting effect. From its perspective, you look back at your childhood and the place you came from and the assumptions you grew up with and they appear trivial and hopeless. You try to compensate by distancing yourself from your origins. At least that was how it went with me. But I still hunted and fished during vacations, with, if possible, a deeper satisfaction than before, and those things always had the effect of extending and deepening my understanding of the world that, like it or not, I had been born into and was now seeing from the outside in, as well as from the inside out.

Because that is another thing about hunting and fishing: nothing—not guns, boats, tackle, or skill in shooting or casting—is more important to them than local knowledge. Now such knowledge has to some extent become a commodity—guides, books, tackle shops, magazines, and web sites are in the business of providing it. But forty years ago, about the only way to acquire it was to know somebody, always older

than yourself, or to simply explore around on your own. Either way, what began as an education about habitats and natural history led to a knowledge of local history and the local economy. You went from knowing that quail liked to roost in the broom straw of old fields to wondering what had been planted in the field and why it had been abandoned; you listened to an old-timer talk about hunting all day through big, open stands of longleaf pine in a section that was now soybean fields interspersed with scruffy thickets of sweet gum, scrub oak, and cat briar. Elsewhere, you would find big pines scarred by turpentining operations from the turn of the century, or the vestige of an old tram road through a swamp, where, you learned, little narrow-gauge locomotives had once chugged to and fro, hauling out pine, cypress, and gum from the bottomlands. I knew two places where there were broken-up vats and scattered cinderblocks, the remnants of somebody's small-scale moonshining operation. And I knew of one place where, when I stopped at the farmhouse to ask to hunt, the farmer always took the trouble to tell me that hit wouldn't be no point atall in my hunting down along the branch behind his lower cornfield; hit mought be best just to keep the dog outen that field altogether. And so I learned that *don't ask, don't tell* was sometimes a corollary of local knowledge.

But the important thing about all of this was that I, a town boy and now on my way to becoming a professional bookworm, gained at least some sense of land use, of the cycles and complications of growing tobacco, which was the basis of the local economy, and of the lives, which were not enviable, of the people who did the growing. And that I learned at least a little about the wide and sometimes rich territory that is neither a human landscape nor a purely natural one, but one created by the ebbing and flowing of human encroachment and natural reclamation over generations. The knowledge was haphazardly acquired and of no practical value, but it served to fortify my connections to a particular and utterly concrete, three-dimensional reality at a time when everything else about my education was tending to weaken those connections.

This sort of local knowledge is not portable—a great specificity about times and places is the essence of it. But having acquired a degree of it about one place has made me feel the need for it in the other places my life has taken me to. If you look at the country around you as a hunter, you are never simply looking at scenery. You are always imagining moving through that landscape, and the promises and possibilities that it may contain within it. The experience is visual and aesthetic, like looking at a painting, but also anticipatory, like looking at the cover of a book you plan one day to open, and read or reread, not so much for what you will get out of it as for what you will experience inside of it: a heightened sense of awareness and suspense, and of so many

things to be noticed, puzzled over, and reconsidered.

FOR THE PAST FEW YEARS, John Lichter has focused a good part of his efforts as a scientist and a teacher on Merrymeeting Bay, and this fall he had a class of Environmental Studies majors looking into the Bay's waterfowl population. I made myself available on every Friday in September to help familiarize them with their subjects. We had half a dozen canoes at our disposal, and there were only a dozen students in the course, so I had a chance to paddle with each of them, and get to know them a little.

All had done a good deal of Environmental Studies work, and a lot of them had already gained familiarity with other aspects of the Bay. None of them had much prior experience with ducks, but they quickly learned to distinguish teal from big ducks, and then blue-winged teal from green-winged teal, and mallards from black ducks. I believe that all of them would have counted themselves as conservationists, and several hoped to find a way, whether as scientists, policymakers, or employees of non-profit organizations, to make conservation their life's work. None were hunters, which did not surprise me. One, Jason, was a serious fly fisherman; another, Andrea, was candidly and courteously unenthusiastic about hunting.

When duck hunting was a bigger business on the Bay, and when the Department of Inland Fisheries and Wildlife

Practicing patience

Prize pupil

had a larger staff of wardens and biologists, the state had fairly good records to indicate how many people hunted there, how successful they were, and how the population of ducks in general and of particular species had fluctuated over the years. But, while the Bay still attracts more ducks and more duck hunters than any other place in Maine, the state no longer has the resources to keep track of them. So, to give our excursions a focus, we tried to agree on a rough estimate of how many ducks we saw on each outing. Because we saw many of the ducks at long distance, we made only one distinction, between teal and big duck. When the ducks were close enough, however, we did try to get a general impression of the ratio of blue-winged teal to green-wings, and of black ducks to mallards.

The results of all this would not amount to science, or have much value. At best, we were establishing an approximate basis of comparison for future reference. I expected that enthusiasm would be highest at the beginning, and would decline sharply, because there wasn't much intellectual challenge in what we were doing, and it was going to be of very limited relevance to the papers the students would eventually need to write and present as their final projects in the course. Time is always a pressing issue for undergraduates, and they dislike using it in ways that are neither purposeful nor cathartic. We tried to make the thing as businesslike as possible, convening at an informal, semiofficial landing near

the Abby mouth at two o'clock sharp, and being back there no later than four. I let it be known that I would be available for early morning expeditions, if anybody preferred to go then, in order to have their Friday afternoons free.

It turned out to be an exceptionally warm September. For the first three weeks, blue-winged teal were in good supply—more than I had seen in years, although still outnumbered two or three to one by green-wings. Their numbers diminished drastically—they are early migrants—in the last week. Teal of both species outnumbered big ducks by a ratio varying between two to one and three to two, and, while we always saw some black ducks, they were scattered individuals within flocks of mallards. On average, we saw seventeen hundred ducks of all species on each outing, although on one early morning trip at low tide, we saw conservatively twice that many, almost all of them teal. Regardless of tide, the birds tended to be concentrated in large flocks, and did not appear to scatter much to feed, which meant that we could paddle past acres of marsh seeing only an occasional duck, and then flush waves of them—three or four hundred at once, followed a minute later by another three or four hundred out of an area half the size of a football field.

The place where we started from each week was the place where Ronnie Burrell had been standing when he saw the eagle and the swan. You get there by turning off a secondary road and onto a tertiary one, which runs through alluvial lowland, most of it wooded. The road is unpaved and narrow, overarched by swamp maples and big pines, so that it feels less like a road than like a lane or path. After three-quarters of a mile, you turn left, onto a sort of driveway, cross a stagnant slough, pass through some more woods, and you are there. You park, walk down a rutted track through a patch of alders, and step out at the edge of the water. There's no ramp, but it is possible, if you are patient, to back a boat trailer through the alders down to the water.

The main channel of the Abby, about forty yards wide, bends in close to shore here. Beyond it lies a lush tidal prairie of wild rice, bulrush, and three-square grass. Directly opposite where you stand and half a mile away is Brown's Point—low, wooded, with a few exceptionally fine-looking fields, with a house or two beyond them. Towering at regular intervals above the trees and the fields are the steel pylons that carry the transmission lines from east Bowdoinham and beyond to the tip of Brown's Point and across the narrow waist of the Bay—the place where the eagle assailed the swan—and so on to Woolwich and beyond. To the left—up the Abby—and a mile away, the prairie is framed by a low causeway and a one-lane bridge, which takes the secondary road northwards toward Richmond. The tip of Brown's Point and the high, darkly wooded, ledgy Woolwich shore frame the view to the right, a mile and a half away. Overhead is an awful lot of sky.

The effect of emerging from the leafy tunnel of the road to this expansive vista—the muddy little tidal river and the wide, shifting grassy sea beyond it—has for me a specific analogy: it is like the effect you get when you walk up from the gloomy, concrete-and-cinderblock concourse of a stadium to come out into the stands, with the sky above you, the light-bathed and brilliantly green diamond and outfield before you, and the sense that the surrounding city, the streets, the traffic, the hubbub, and the whole disenchanting, unforgiving, steel-and-brick-and-asphalt reality of it has been whisked away and replaced by this self-contained amphitheater, where the air is alive with a magical possibility. You lose yourself, just for a moment.

Well, that is how it seems to me now, when I come down Center Point to the Abby. It's a feeling that has deepened with recurrence, and I like it a lot. But it isn't the sort of thing you blather about, except on paper, and it especially isn't the sort of thing you blather about to a bunch of bright undergraduates of a scientific bent. The first day there, we got the canoes off the trailer and lugged them down to the water, reviewed a few basic things about ducks, wild rice, and the Bay in general, and, like a stewardess at the beginning of a flight, I recited the mandatory platitudes about life-preservers, canoe safety, how to turn a canoe into the wind, what to do in the unlikely event of a water landing, blah, blah, blah. Then, as best we could, we paired experienced paddlers with inexperienced ones, and semiexperienced ones with each other, and set out in the general direction of the pylons at the end of Brown's Point. We kept close together, and started seeing ducks within a few hundred yards—mostly small groups of blue-winged teal, fifteen or twenty at a time, easy to identify and easy to count.

On that initial outing and all the subsequent ones, we found most of the ducks out near the end of Brown's Point, where the Abby delta encounters the Kennebec channel and concludes. That was good, particularly when we had a half tide—the sculler's tide, the harrier's tide. There are all sorts of small and smaller veins and capillaries of water through the marsh, connecting the main channel of the Abby to the Kennebec. Paddling these, even without the ducks, is fun. Some are only a little wider than a canoe and barely deep enough to float it; when you are seated, you cannot see over the rice, and so you are *inside* the marsh. The runnels of water sometimes play out; sometimes they connect to others, widening as you approach the Kennebec. It's a bit of a maze, with dead ends and concealed openings. Sometimes we'd round a corner and flush a few teal from the channel, but most flushed from the marsh beside us, in groups and gangs big enough to make a roar when they took off.

I knew how I felt—how I always feel—about this: like a rich man, like a boy, and so forth. But I did not know what the younger generation would make of it. As a species, we must mutate from one generation to the next, because our environment—the economic, technological, cultural, political, temporal determinants of our lives—alters incessantly and rapidly, and the alterations are cumulative. It is nice to think of that kind of environment as being secondary, artificial, and superficial, and to declare that the primary and profound one was represented by what we were paddling through—air, water, geography, biology, birds, fish, weather, and all the other ahistorical entities and processes. But, whatever its metaphysical status, the secondary environment gives us the houses we live in, the language we think in, the assumptions that shape our thinking, the primary objects of our fear or desire, the daily realities we confront or shun or shirk from. We have no selves and are nobody without it.

That secondary environment had changed enormously from my life to theirs, and one of the things that had changed in it was childhood—how it was experienced and how it was remembered. Theirs would have included a lot less unscheduled idleness, a lot less *faut de mieux* knocking around, poking around, reading around, turning over logs, looking under them, and improvising an imagination in the process. Complex, challenging games of hide-and-seek, tag, search-and-destroy existed for them in virtual form, educating them into a kind of literacy—which is a kind of reality—that possibly resembled the old one in its complexity, but not in its effects and its relation to memory. The childhood I remembered would be to the one they remembered as the one my grandmother remembered had been to mine: something of antiquarian or anthropological interest, quaint or estimable or appealing, perhaps, but, in terms of their present, past, or future, unreal.

It is a matter of how a particular generation connects its secondary world to the primary one, and how far apart the two are to start with. My secondary world included a lot of books that all tended in the same direction—*Robinson Crusoe, The Adventures of Huckleberry Finn, The Deerslayer, The Swiss Family Robinson, The Call of the Wild, The Little House on the Prairie, The Wind and the Willows.* These books had the status of childhood classics (which meant, among other things, that my first acquaintance with them was sometimes in comic book form). Behind them lay shoals and flocks and swarms of lesser books, stories, magazine articles, movies, and radio programs like *Sergeant Preston of the Yukon* and *Mark Trail*—the pervasive ephemera of popular culture. Their narratives connected geography and discovery, geography and adventure; they emphasized solitude and discommended the dismal regularities of civilized and secondary environments—including, of course, the one shared by writers, publishers, books, booksellers, and readers, but never mind. They sent me straight out into the nearest version of the primary environment I could find, and as deep into it, psychologically as well as physically, as I could get; and away from the tedium, compli-

cation, scrutiny, discipline, and calculation that were apparently necessary if I were to become a functional adult.

Talking with these particular students, I could not deduce what narratives and fantasies had replaced the ones I grew up with. Theirs may be no less escapist, but certainly they are different. I suspected that they were predicated less on the Edenic possibilities of the natural world, and therefore less elegiac and retrospective, more oriented to the future, and to utopian or dystopian possibilities in the secondary world. In part, this was simply a reflection of the fact that, between my childhood and theirs, the dimensions and power of the natural world had shrunk, making it more and more an annex of the human one—it was perhaps a place to be loved, looked after, enjoyed, preserved; but therefore a place requiring you to exercise your civic sense of responsibility, not a refuge from it.

I asked this student and that where they were from, how they'd gotten interested in environmental matters, how that interest jibed with their other interests. Their answers were lucid, sensible, and largely impersonal. That is how education teaches you to answer questions and is no doubt how I would have answered any such queries if they had been put to me when I was an undergraduate. Given Bowdoin's demography, a surprising number of students were from the West—Colorado, Oregon, Washington, and places like that. They had hiked, skied, or sailed. One, from Florida, had

Linwood Rideout

Ronnie Burrell

Ronnie Burrell going about his business

Buster Prout. The gunning float is the first he built, more than forty years ago.

spent a lot of time pushing and paddling himself around in the Everglades, photographing birds. One, although a New Englander, had found a way to spend a year in Montana; one had studied in France. Their horizons were plenty broad; they traveled easily and eagerly, unencumbered by provincialism, or at least unaware of it.

We talked, we paddled, we flushed ducks and counted them. We flushed harriers and found the remains of teal they'd caught, and twice we saw a peregrine. Eagles were about. And the conversation flagged in direct and gratifying proportion to the number of ducks in the air. Teal were the show-stoppers, the conversation-killers, sometimes swerving with the coordinated precision of sandpipers or a school of fish, flaring, wheeling, dipping, and lifting in unison, just over the tips of the rice, their white bellies suddenly flashing, then disappearing, like semaphore signals. We'd venture our guesses about the size of the flock, but mostly just watch. John Lichter had said to me that the real purpose of these expeditions was to get the students fired up about the projects they would be doing, and with one or two exceptions, of the sort that might be taken as unscientific proof of the rule, that was what was happening. The interest and enthusiasm grew instead of waning, and the early morning trips became more popular, not because they left Friday afternoons unencumbered, but because word got around that you saw more birds then, and got closer to them.

So somehow a good connection was taking place between their secondary worlds and our primary one—they were catching for themselves and on their own terms something of the excitement and pleasure that teachers cannot teach, but perhaps can unintentionally share.

At the end of September, we took our last paddle—it was time for them to start defining and settling down to their projects, and for me to get down to hunting. In preparing the course, John Lichter had realized that there was a dearth of reliable data, and had consulted a lot of unscientific sources, trying to find connections or disparities between such data as existed and more impressionistic, less quantified data—published memoirs, local histories, and living memory. To this end, he'd asked me to get in touch with the senior generation of active, lifelong hunters around the Bay, and to ask them to keep a log of their hunts—recording not simply how often they'd gone out and how successful they'd been, but also noting down anything that seemed characteristic or interesting about this season—how many ducks they saw, where they saw them, anything about them, or the Bay itself, that seemed different from the recent or more distant past. I was glad to do this, and also to arrange for the students and the hunters to meet early in November, after the first half of the duck season had ended, and to talk things over.

THE SEVEN HUNTERS WHO PARTICIPATED COLLECTIVELY represented something more than two and a half centuries of gunning on the Bay, guiding on it, fishing on it, trapping around its borders, and simply keeping an eye on it. They were Ronnie Burrell, Richard Nickerson, Buster Prout, Jim Brawn, Adelbert Temple, John Edgecomb, and Harold Nickerson. I have listed them in approximate order of seniority. The Nickersons—father and son—are from Brunswick, the others from Bowdoinham, although they would have gone to junior high and high school in Brunswick, under an arrangement that existed until the early seventies. So they know each other, and share a good many things besides hunting. I think Buster is the only one of them who was not introduced to hunting first and foremost by his father; I have the impression that Ronnie, who at seventy-six is about a dozen years his senior, assumed that role in his life. The two of them still hunt together and guide together, a partnership that goes back for half a century. Buster built his first gunning float forty-five years ago. He still builds them, and is acknowledged by everyone but himself to have brought that local art to its highest level of development. But most of the other men have built floats for themselves—more on that later. Ronnie Burrell speaks of his float the way he speaks of a lot of things, with telegraphic brevity and self-deprecating irreverence: "You'll have to come over and see that float I built.

Course you'll have to come at low tide."

John Edgecomb fiberglasses the floats that Buster builds. Jim Brawn is John Edgecomb's uncle. John built the float that Adelbert uses, as well as his own, and the two of them hunt together for much of the season. Adelbert and Jim Brawn bowl together in a local league. To the considerable extent that their memories are collective and intertwined, each man serves as the other's fact-checker. Perhaps for that reason, the telling of tall tales and big stories is not part of their hunting culture, as it was of the one I grew up in. And their memories are not confined to their experience, long as that experience is. Ronnie will comment in passing about how much shallower and more obstructed by logs the Abby is now than when his grandfather used to make some significant seasonal money drift netting shad there. John Edgecomb mentions that his grandfather netted suckers through the ice in the winter, to sell for smelt fishermen to cut up and use as bait. The Nickersons own a local storage and moving company that was begun when Richard's great-grandfather got himself a tugboat and a scow to lighter coal from Bath up to Brunswick: "We didn't get into the trucking part of it until, oh, I don't know, 1919, I think it was." The tug and the scow rode the rising tide up to Brunswick, and the falling water back to Bath. "That tug going back and forth kept a pretty good channel busted out through the Androscoggin mouth," Richard says. "Wish I had me one of them," says Ronnie.

Richard started hunting when he was five, but says he wasn't much good at it until he was about eight or nine. He has photographs of himself as a boy with his father, and of his father as a boy with his grandfather, and his grandfather as a boy with his great-grandfather. Shotguns and dead waterfowl figure prominently in each of these images. His own son Harold started hunting at about the same age Richard himself had, when he was still too young to have a hunting license or handle a shotgun. Richard equipped him with a BB gun—training wheels, so to speak—and they went out together, the little boy in the front of the float, dead serious—an acolyte, an apprentice, an understudy to a heritage.

Buster and Ronnie both live on Abagadasset Road, and grew up beside the Abby. Their stomping grounds are the middle and upper Bay—the Abby and its mouth; the Foot—the marsh at the downstream end of Swan Island; and the Big Flats—the marsh that extends upstream from the Eastern River mouth. If asked to rate the different ways of hunting ducks, they would say they like them all, and I would say that they are superlatively good at all of them. But they would also say that hunting over decoys is their least favorite way to do it. The others do much the greater part of their hunting over decoys. This may have to do with the fact that Ronnie and Buster have, since their late teens, done a great deal of guiding on the Bay, and always understood that to mean that when you hunted ducks you *hunted* them; you did

not simply sit and wait for them to come to you.

The others have the Androscoggin mouth and the lower Bay as their primary base of operations. John, Jim, and the Nickersons have camps there, almost abutting each other. These are one-room buildings squeezed in between the road and the water out near the end of Pleasant Point, in Topsham. These camps were originally pretty rough-and-ready affairs, but they have over the years been tidied up, improved, and turned into neat, pleasing places—snug without being cluttered, trim without being fussy. Each has its small dock, running from the ledge on which the houses are perched down to the water, ten or fifteen feet below. Their floats are moored off the end of the docks, on haul-out rigs that operate on pulleys, like those clotheslines that used to be strung between apartment buildings.

If you see one of the lower Bay hunters motoring across the Androscoggin mouth, or headed down it and out into the Bay, or up it toward some of the promising marshes in that direction, you think nothing of it—a man or two in a small boat with a small motor, chugging along one edge, the other edge, or somewhere out in the middle of a river mouth that is, in front of their camps, at least a mile wide. You think nothing of it unless you've tried it yourself, that is. If you have tried it yourself, you watch carefully, and, for the sake of your own self-esteem, you hope to see one of them suddenly stop, or abruptly change directions, or, better yet, shut off the motor, tilt it up, and start poling. You don't see that; you won't see that. Jim Brawn once watched from the deck of his camp as a moose crossed the river here. "She had to swim for a few yards, way over on the other side," he said. Ronnie did not believe him; Ronnie was sure that a woodchuck could cross the Androscoggin there and not have to swim.

So Buster and Ronnie, and particularly Ronnie, have as little to do with the Androscoggin mouth as possible, while Richard Nickerson almost never hunts anywhere else. Ronnie tells a story from years ago, about a sport he guided who was renting a camp somewhere on Pleasant Point. It was high tide first thing in the morning, so Ronnie motored down from the Abby, picked him up, and they went back and hunted around the Abby mouth until midday. The sport wanted to have lunch back in his camp, and told Ronnie to take him there—on low tide.

"We'll just go back to my place and you can call, get somebody to come pick you up," said Ronnie.

The sport said that wouldn't work—there was nobody there to come and get him. And it didn't make sense any-way—why not just go back by boat?

"Tell you what," said Ronnie, "We'll go back to my place and I'll run you over there in my truck."

The sport said that didn't make sense either. Why not just go back in the boat? He *wanted* to go back by boat.

He would enjoy the ride.

"You want to go by boat to Pleasant Point at low tide." Ronnie did not ask this but stated it, in the manner of a court official taking a deposition, reading back to the witness what the witness had said to him.

"Yes," said the sport. "I *want* to go *by boat*. To *Pleasant Point*. For *lunch*."

"Good," said Ronnie. "Here's what we'll do. We'll go back to my place. We'll put the boat in the back of my truck. I'll drive the truck, and you can go by boat."

The hunters, then, have their territories. I don't think they feel that their preferred parts of the Bay belong to them, in even the slightest sense, or that they would in the slightest sense feel themselves to be trespassing on other parts of the Bay. It is more a matter of familiarity, associa-tions, and connections. One morning Jim Brawn and I were out in Willis Cove, across from Pleasant Point. I'd never hunted there, and said so. Jim said he actually felt a little funny hunting there himself—he'd grown up doing most of his hunting around the Cathance mouth, Muddy River mouth, and up both those rivers. He hadn't really started hunting the Androscoggin until after he'd retired from the military and come back home. I asked him how long ago that was. Twenty years or so, he said—not even a third of a single lifetime, as opposed to two or three generations.

Linwood Rideout, dean of the Bay's duck guides and archive of its history

So THESE WERE THE MEN who came into Druckenmiller Hall on the northeast corner of the Bowdoin campus to meet with a dozen undergraduates, John Lichter, and myself on a warmish night in early November. I rode in with Buster, Ronnie, and Jim. I told Ronnie I didn't see why we couldn't have gone to Brunswick by boat, up the Androscoggin, just to hear him snort and tell that story again. And I hoped to myself that everything would go all right this evening—there was a pretty big discrepancy between the secondary worlds that were going to be trying to communicate with each other there in a seminar room. It occurred to me that even after forty years of being in and around colleges, I found a science building an uncomfortable sort of place, with incomprehensible charts and posters on the walls of the hallways, and laboratories visible through glass doors, and something of the hygienic, bland menace of a hospital. I wasn't at all sure what the hunters would make of it, or how comfortable they'd be with the students, or the students with them.

It turned out fine. To start us off, I asked John Edgecomb to talk about his general impressions of the first duck season, which had just ended. He and I had talked a good deal during October, and I knew he'd seen some things that interested him. And so he talked about hunting over on Willis Cove with Adelbert and noticing an unusual amount of uprooted vegetation floating in the water and getting caught on the decoy lines. They'd looked at it and recognized it as a subsurface plant that grows here and there in the sandy shallows of the Androscoggin mouth. John had taken some home, used the Internet, and figured out that it was probably wild celery, an important duck food but not one that had been common enough to be considered significant on the Bay—at least, not during his lifetime as a hunter.

Joshua, the fly-fishing student, had been looking at the contents of duck stomachs that a few of us had provided him with. He and John Lichter confirmed John Edgecomb's deduction—the plant was wild celery and the ducks had been eating it. Feeding on it allowed them to stay on open water out in the Androscoggin mouth, where nothing could approach them, so while it might or might not have had the nutritional value of wild rice, it was, from the duck's standpoint, a much *healthier* food. Apparently it was increasing—John had never before seen much evidence that ducks ate it, nor had Adelbert or any of the rest of us.

And then the conversation became general—ducks, duck food, duck habits, duck habitat at present, in the recent, and the less-recent past, and changes in the tide flats and channels. Diving ducks—what had happened to the whistlers? Might the celery bring them back? Black ducks—were more of them spending the fall down on Maquoit Bay and elsewhere along the coast than in the past? Was that the case with geese too? Why had ducks stopped coming into the Bay in big numbers late in the afternoon, to spend the night there? Buster talked about himself and his brother as boys, standing on the flat roof of the entryway to the farmhouse where they grew up, and looking down the Abby toward the Bay: "Thousands of ducks. I'd hesitate to say exactly how many, because it was almost too many to believe. It seemed endless, just *streaming* into that Bay at dusk. Sometimes teal, but mostly blacks. It was a thing to see; it almost don't seem possible now."

I think some of it went over the students' heads, because some of it went over mine. The hunters were all so familiar with what they were talking about, and they talked with great specificity—the Chain Rock, Buttermilk Channel, the Eastern Lookout, the Foot, the Flats, the Sands, the Horseshoe, Beech Creek, Pogue's Hole, Maxwell Island, Windmill Cove, Alder Point—places that don't show up on maps, and aren't always known, even among the hunters themselves, by the same names. They talked about Opening Day back in the fifties, when there'd be hunters spaced out every hundred yards or so along the breakwater at the Eastern River mouth, and everybody getting shooting, and the same thing down along the edge of Willis Cove. Somebody mentioned Linwood Rideout, who'd been the helmsman of an LCI at Normandy, shuttling troops back and forth under a barrage of artillery, mortar, and small-arms fire; and how Linwood had said that it had been pretty noisy there, like an extra good

Opening Day. It was nothing like that now, and especially not this year. Ronnie, in one of his patented asides, said, "Well, this wurn't the worst Openin' Day I ever saw. T'wur about half that good."

At first I felt like a sheepdog that had stumbled upon a bunch of deer and presumed that they needed to be herded together and all headed in the same direction at the same time. But I looked over at John Lichter and he had the look of a teacher who was enjoying himself, and relishing what was happening. It was his class, and if he was willing to have the conversation go running off in five directions at once, then I certainly wasn't going to interfere. Richard Nickerson talked about his high-school years, back in the fifties, and how on Opening Day most of the boys brought their shotguns to school with them. They'd be let out of class at noon, so they could head for the Bay. He laughed, "Reason the principal let us out was he'd be going gunning himself. Nobody worried about the guns—just stick 'em in the lockers, and the lockers didn't even have locks on 'em. Sometimes my dad would come in from the morning shoot and pick me up to go out with him, but a lot of times we'd just walk around the edge of the Bay, slog out onto the flats if the tide was low, get our limit that way. It was an awful lot of birds then—it seemed like there wouldn't have been room for 'em, if there'd been any more."

Joshua had brought along a dish of seeds he'd removed

from duck gizzards, that neither he nor John Lichter could identify. He passed it around, and everybody looked and ventured an opinion—definitely not a marsh plant or an underwater plant; something that grew on the shore, just above the tide line; so much rain this fall, the rivers and the Bay so high, the ducks were feeding on all sorts of different things this year. One of the students wondered if that meant that wild rice wasn't as important a duck food as was commonly assumed. That was youthful heresy, and Richard catechized her:

"If you had steak and you had baloney, which would you eat?"

She sensed a trap, and looked a little wary. "Steak?"

"Right. Now, if you had baloney and you had nothing, which would you eat?"

She saw it now and laughed.

"What you're saying is *that*"—she pointed at the dish with the mystery seeds—"is a bunch of baloney?"

He laughed, too. "Right. Water's so high they can't get at the rice, except for a little while at low tide. So they're making do with baloney."

And so that was how it went—an evening that was a social success of the sort that is and of itself educative. The talk edged for a while toward the question of hunting and conservation. John Edgecomb was much of Thoreau's opinion—that hunters were the best friends ducks had. "Other people don't want ducks to go extinct or anything like that. But hunters have been the ones to raise the money and save the nesting grounds. They're the ones who know and care about how many ducks there used to be. They want to see that many ducks again." Buster, quiet as always, said to the students what I have heard him say on more than one occasion. "There's a lot more to it than killing ducks. You go out there, you see eagles, you see the sun rise. If it was just killin' something, I would have stopped a long time ago—might not have started at all." One student asked how they'd come to take up duck hunting at all. It seemed to me obvious—surely it was evident that these men didn't *take up* hunting in the way that Jim and Adelbert, for example, had taken up bowling. They were born into it—it was like asking them why they had taken up speaking the language they spoke in the way that they spoke it. But the question led them to talk about something that plainly concerned them—you didn't see many young people at all out on the Bay now. The state had introduced a special Youth Day—a one-day duck season that was held a week before the regular season; only hunters who were under 16, and who were accompanied by an adult with a hunting license, were allowed to shoot. Buster, Ronnie, and a lot of the others always took a boy out on that day, and it seemed to them that the boys enjoyed it, but just as a neat thing to do. One had cancelled at the last minute this year, because he had a soccer match. Everybody shook their heads at that—it implied a set of priorities, a secondary world, that was not only different from their own, but also different from that of their fathers and grandfathers.

We were ending up now. Adelbert had been sitting next to John Edgecomb, up at one end of the table, and he hadn't said much all evening, but he'd looked perfectly comfortable with himself and the situation, watching and listening. As the students were starting to gather up their notebooks and push their chairs back from the table, he spoke in a musing kind of way, as though thinking aloud:

"Used to be, some high-school kid sitting in class, staring out the window, and I'd be pretty sure I knew right what he was thinking about. I'd probably be thinking about it, too, to tell you the truth. But now? I got no idea. I got no idea in this world what's on that kid's mind."

OGL and the OED

A FRINGE BENEFIT OF MERRYMEETING BAY is the language you hear spoken around it. It's often what a friend from South Carolina calls Old Growth Language, which is a good way to think of it: something deeply rooted, in a location that hasn't been drastically disturbed for a long time; something less frequently met in the present than in the past, and that may not be met with at all in the future.

You are likeliest to find OGL where speakers of English have lived and interacted with their environments and each other for at least a couple of centuries, in circumstances that have not attracted a great deal of in-migration. Surprisingly often, its roots are in British English—words, usages, and pronunciations that have dropped out of contemporary British speech, or that, if they do survive, are peculiar to particular regions of the island, or particular trades or particular social groups, like sailors or country squires or urban guttersnipes. You discover this by consulting, first and foremost, the better than fifteen thousand, triple-columned pages of the thirteen-volume *Oxford English Dictionary* (*OED*). That usually does the job, although you generally should check the four-volume *Dictionary of American Regional English* (*DARE*) as well. "Words," said Samuel Johnson, "are the daughters of the earth, but things are the sons of heaven." I am not quite sure how to take that, except that it implies that words and things are both elemental and mysterious, and their relationship (kissing cousins? strange bedfellows?) invites conjecture.

I first ran into the local version of OGL when I was still new to Maine and Maine was still new to me. I was at the town landing in Bowdoinham and heard one duck hunter, who had just come in from a morning on the Bay, tell another, who was just headed out:

"There's a [*huh? what?*] of birds out there."
My hearing was good in those days. A *pa sill* of birds? A *pause ull* of them? Some arcane nautical or architectural lingo? Then I realized that, for the sake of emphasis, the hunter had prolonged a two-syllable word in pronouncing it, so it sounded like two monosyllables; and that the original disyllable was intermediate between the familiar folksy colloquialism *passel* and the Standard English *parcel*. And that was how, when, and where I first recognized that *passel* was just a different pronunciation of *parcel*. Something about the way the hunter dropped the *r* left a sort of aural footprint on the first syllable—evidence that it had formerly been there.

One reason it had never occurred to me that *parcel* and *passel* are the same word was that their meanings appear to be the opposite of each other. A *passel* is a bunch, a gang, a crowd, a crew, a pack—a collection of things. A *parcel* is a

single item—a package you get from the post office, for example—or a portion of a larger item, as in a *parcel* of land: a tract taken out of a larger tract. In the *OED* I discovered:

A) that the primary meaning of *parcel* has always been about what it still is—a single thing, or a part of it;

B) that *parcel* had also had a secondary meaning, designating a group of things—a *passel* of things, in other words;

1) that the secondary meaning was now obsolete, except in certain regional dialects;

2) that this secondary meaning was quite often used in connection with birds. *The Oxford English Dictionary* cites references to:

a) a *parcel* of crows;

b) a *parcel* of linnets;

c) a *parcel* of penguins. Which sounds like something your true love might give to you if Christmas had a thirteenth day.

OGL can have a sweet formality about it, because you hear in it words you'd previously found only in print. Linwood Rideout speaks naturally and easily of going out on the Bay in the *forenoon*; and he once approvingly said of a boat that it was *capable*. That sounds as though he was giving the boat a human characteristic, but he was not. He was using the word in its old sense of *capacious*. When applied to watercraft, the word carries the additional sense of *seaworthy*—presumably even when fully loaded. David Berry will refer to a scrawny, bedraggled old hen as *spleeny*—down with a bad case of anemia, hypochondria, or the dumps. That is a variant of *splenetic*, and takes us back to the art and science of medical diagnostics as they existed four or five hundred years ago. Ronnie Burrell, who deploys OGL with judicious distinction, will come into your house on a cold night and go stand beside the wood stove for a few minutes, to get the chill off. He'll ask you some questions about the stove—he's a woodcutter, heats his house with wood, and is interested in such matters. Then he'll spread his hands out over it the way anybody would, to catch that almost palpable heat.

"Well," he says, "she's *testifying* tonight, and that's for sure."

That's a metaphor, with the riddle-like quality a good metaphor has: how does a roaring wood stove resemble a true believer?—by its ardor, its fervor, its radiant heat. The analogy affectionately anthropomorphizes the stove, and mixes cool detachment and some admiration into its attitude toward the ecstatic public declaration of religious rapture. I don't imagine Ronnie coined the metaphor—it probably went back to one or another of the Christian/Populist Great Awakenings of New England; but its salty independence of attitude preserves its pith and freshness, and makes it pretty expressive of Ronnie himself.

Out on the Bay, *sheldrake* is the usual name for the common merganser (a species that occurs throughout the

Sheldrake

northerly latitudes of North America and Eurasia, and is known in England as the goosander). Among ornithologists, *sheldrake* properly applies to *Tandorna tandorna*—a big European saltwater duck that has no equivalent on this side of the Atlantic. The European sheldrake does not resemble the merganser in its habits or physique, but does in its habitat and the pattern of its plumage. When British colonists in this country found birds here that even superficially resembled birds they'd grown up with, they often called them by that name—hence the great difference between the birds we know as robins, blackbirds, larks, partridges, and so forth, and the ones that are called the same thing in England. A hundred and seventy-five years ago, John James Audubon called mergansers mergansers, but noted that they were referred to as sheldrakes by most Americans. That has largely died out now—even the oldest gunners in South Carolina did not call mergansers sheldrakes when I was growing up there, although they had a variety of other names for them, none of them respectful. But the old moniker, a distant echo of England, still survives in these parts.

I have heard Buster and others refer to the hooded merganser as a *picket bill*. I haven't run across this nickname anywhere else. It uses *picket* in its oldest and strictest sense—as the diminutive of the word *pike*, and thus a small, slender spike or stake. The hooded merganser's beak is thin in relation to the rest of the bird, and the bird itself is by much the smallest of the three North American mergansers, and so the diminutive fits it snugly. It is also a dapper, lively little bird, usually traveling in a flock of eight or ten. On the water, they splash around a good deal, chase each other, and aren't especially wary; you can sometimes scull to within a boat-length of them before they notice, and react exactly as an unruly class of grammar schoolers would when the teacher unexpectedly walks in—every head pops up in unison, and every bird begins to fidget nervously. *Picket bill*, just as a name, seems to me to be like the names of some flowers—*Johnny jump-up*, say, or *beggars' lice*—in having the teasing, apt familiarity of a good nickname, as though it were what William Pitt's pals called him. Itty-bittiness echoes behind all those short *i*'s.

Here are some other examples of OGL, all closely associated with the Bay and used routinely by native speakers:

1. *Chops* (noun). This one seemed to be a no-brainer. The Chops is the narrow, deep channel between North Bath and Woolwich, where the whole Androscoggin-Kennebec watershed funnels out of the Bay. When the tide is running strongly, it forms powerful rips and countercurrents. If it's breezy, the already turbulent surface becomes a lot more turbulent, with a very uneven wave pattern caused by the wind's blowing with some currents and against others. If you are in a small boat, getting yourself yanked and buffeted and

soaked, you have no trouble convincing yourself that the Chops owes its name to its choppiness.

But one day I happened on an early nineteenth-century map of the lower Kennebec in the Bowdoin College Archives, and noticed that it referred to the Chops as the *Chaps*, and that, I knew, once meant *jaws*. The poet Andrew Marvell had famously used it that way in "To His Coy Mistress" (1678), warning his girlfriend of "Time's slow-chapped power"—it would make short work of youth and beauty, and so he and she shouldn't shilly-shally. In more or less modern usage—maybe a gangster movie from forty or fifty years ago—a tough guy, facing the same situation that Marvell faced, but less genteel in addressing it, might threaten to give the non-compliant dame a smack across the *chops*—a hard slap in the mouth.

In the *OED*, I found that *chops*, when used figuratively and in relation to landscape, basically referred to a narrow passageway, like an alpine gap or valley. More to the point, the south end of the English Channel, where it widens out into the Atlantic Ocean, was familiarly known to British sailors and the Lords of the Admiralty as the *Chops of the Channel*. The term was also used generically for any narrow nautical passageway between rocky shores. But undoubtedly for English people, the term chiefly evoked the stretch of water between Cornwall and Brittany. Alliteration gave *Chops* and *Channel* a kind of inevitability; a history of seafaring and

shipwrecks, of departures from the great port of London and returns to it through this perilous stretch of water gave it notoriety. *The* Chops, *the* Channel—no need to identify them further, in the same way that, when you live in Bowdoinham, you don't need to explain which bay you are talking about when you refer to *the* Bay.

Of course the usual name for a place where a narrower body of water opens out into a larger one, is a *mouth*. But *mouth* has quite a different connotation from *jaw* or *chop*. Jaws are studded with teeth and operated by powerful muscles. They may grind, chomp, champ, clench, and otherwise abuse whatever enters them. Mouths, by comparison, are less threatening, and can be used for such gentle purposes as articulation and osculation—the purposes for which Andrew Marvell used, and hoped to use, his. The Kennebec mouth is lipped by Popham Beach, and does not look particularly threatening. The Chops is another story.

The Chops of the Channel, dangerous at any time, and doubly dangerous in time of war when it became the jaws of death—a place of ambush, without much maneuvering room, a hard place for a fleet to sail into or out of if there were some good sailors determined to stop it—was very well fixed in English memory, and a lot of the early settlers in this section of the New World would have sailed out through it, some gladly, some sadly, but all, no doubt, knowing the fearsome reputation of the place among seafarers. I am guessing that when some of those people came up the Kennebec through that narrow passage, and out into the unexpected expanse of the Bay, they thought of it as a kind of miniature of the Chops of the Channel. They planted the familiar name in the unfamiliar place, in about the way that a group of soldiers from Manhattan might call the muddy main thoroughfare of their encampment *Broadway*, with a mixture of homesickness and sarcasm.

2. *Guzzle* (noun). My *American Heritage Dictionary of the English Language* (Third Edition) boasts 350,000 entries and implies that it is just about the last word on the American vocabulary. It lists *guzzle* as a verb, the one we use to describe how fraternity boys and SUVs satisfy their thirsts. But it does not list it as a noun.

Around the Bay, a *guzzle* is a small creek or channel going through or at least up into a tide flat. Everybody agrees on that. It may also refer to a narrow stream that runs back up into a wooded swamp, although I notice that some hunters—Buster Prout, for example—refer to that sort of place as a *crick*, as distinguished from a guzzle.

The sound of the word and its meaning as a verb suggest its kinship with words like *gizzard, gullet* and *gut*. And so if you enter the Kennebec *mouth*, pass up through the *Chops*, and then push up one of the *guzzles* that makes in toward Pleasant Point, your beautiful trip is following a rather unpleasant logic of ingestion, mastication, and digestion. The *OED* does list *guzzle* as a noun—an obsolete one. It could refer to the throat, but it normally meant something like a gutter or an open sewer—the sort of filthy little drain or ditch that ran along the edges of the unpaved streets of London, or through a pigsty. Zealous converts, when testifying to their own redemption, liked to refer to the *guzzle of depravity* from which Divine Grace had rescued them.

But in the New World—at least in the New England portion of it—a guzzle was, in general, a tidal creek. I can't find any evidence that the word was used much further south than Long Island. In the more southerly part of its range—Cape Cod, for example—it generally referred to a narrow, shallow channel that ran across a beach, draining a low area behind it, or that ran behind a beach, cutting it off from the mainland at high tide. In South Carolina, the term for that sort of inlet or back channel was a *swash*—a piece of OGL from a different ecosystem. It appears that the less restricted way that *guzzle* is used around the Bay is consistent with the way that it is used further Down East and on up into the Maritime Provinces—having so few beaches, perhaps people in those areas had to find other employment for the word.

3. *The Grass* (noun). You almost never hear the older hunters around the Bay talk about marshes. They speak instead of *the grass*. Wild rice is of course a grass and it predominates the Bay's marshes. The predominant plants of other kinds of freshwater or saltwater marshes—bulrush,

Pushing the grass

fragmites, spartina, cattails, and so forth—are not grasses, so there is a certain botanical aptness involved in this idiom. But I expect that is accidental. In England, *the grass* was used by the sporting gentry to designate a hunting field, a place that was good habitat for partridge and pheasant, and that seems to me the likeliest origin of the local use of it. In any event, I like it very much—it insists on the difference between the vegetation and general appearance of the tide flats on the Bay and those of any other marsh.

I also like it because the King James Bible tells us that all flesh is grass—grass, even more than bread, is the staff of life, because so many of the wild and domestic animals that we eat eat it. And around the Bay, the marshes of wild rice have that kind of basic, life-sustaining importance—the staff of much local life, its annual crop closely observed and much commented upon by hunters.

I've never read or heard of any other locality where marshland vegetation in general, or wild rice in particular, is referred to in this way.

4. *Float* (noun, almost invariably modified: *gunning float*). When the Normans conquered England in 1066, they brought with them their own language, which was French. The language of the conquered people was Germanic. The two languages gradually merged, and in this process some words of the old Germanic vocabulary underwent a kind of demotion. For example, the Old English word *stol* referred to the piece of furniture that a king sat on. It was replaced by the French word *trone*. Our words *stool* and *throne* descend from these, but of course *stool* now refers to something you would sit on to milk a cow, but not to rule a kingdom.

Float, as a noun, suffered the same fate that *stol* did. Twelve hundred years ago, in the great Old English epic poem *Beowulf*, a *flota* was a ship—specifically a slender, swift, double-ended, clinker-built, high-prowed longboat, of the type we usually associate with the Vikings. From the standpoint of grace and beauty, not many boats, ancient or modern, exceed it; and from the standpoint of naval architecture, it represented the state of the art in its own time. But in the centuries after the Norman Conquest, *flota* or *float* came to refer to the most rudimentary type of watercraft imaginable—a barge, a scow, or simply a raft. For the last five or six centuries, when the word is used with reference to a boat, that is the kind of boat it refers to: a seagoing shoebox.

The boats hunters use around the Bay are always called *gunning floats*, and they are not at all boxy, raftlike, or crude. They are streamlined and curvilinear, made to slip through the water and the grass with a minimum of friction and noise. How did they come to have a name that does them no justice at all?

I would be very happy to announce to you that this was because somehow the original, Old English sense of *flota* had survived, and that a fragment of the language of *Beowulf* was still current among us. That would be Old Growth Language indeed. But there is no evidence to support that.

More likely, the first gunning floats were crude affairs— probably narrow, flat-bottomed, square-ended scows, suitable for poling. In England, boats of this type are generally called *punts*, but the *OED* indicates that in Ireland, they seem to have been called *floats*, and used in hunting waterfowl. In the vicinity of Merrymeeting Bay, with its great tradition of boat- and shipbuilding, the simple design was progressively modified to suit local conditions, and gradually evolved into the strange, low-profile and shapely little boats that we have now—they are worth an essay in themselves, and they will get it. If you've ever used one as it was designed to be used, you've had yourself a nice experience in the fusion of form and function.

The men who build these boats refer to them rather disparagingly, as though they still thought of them as being as rudimentary and clunky as a milking stool. I think this is just the regional habit of understatement, a rigid avoidance of pretension. The rudimentary boat evolved; the unflattering word assigned to it did not. As far as I know, there has been only one exception to this rule. Bun Carter, an old guide who died a few years ago, once had the bright idea of building a gunning float that would be wide enough to accommodate two sports, sitting side by side, in the front. To be that wide and still be scullable, it also had to be a lot longer than the typical float. He obviously figured that, with such a rig, he could more or less double his *per diem* charges, and make out like a bandit. There are a lot of funny stories told around the Bay at the expense of that boat. In them, the boat itself is almost a character, and she is known exclusively by either of two names. One is *Queen Mary.* The other is *Leviathan.*

5. *Push* (verb). In standard usage, *to push* has a fairly wide range of applications, and if, for example, you overheard someone talking about *pushing grass*, you might reasonably suspect him of drug trafficking. But around the Bay, *pushing* the grass, or *pushing* Butler Cove means standing in the back of a gunning float and using the long sculling oar to pole it through the wild rice, in hopes of jumping a duck. This seems obvious enough, but two things about it are curious: 1) why not just say *pole*, which is more precise than *push*? 2) shouldn't it be push *through* the grass, with the gunning float being understood as the direct object—the thing that's being pushed? *Push the grass* makes it sound as though you are shoving the grass along, instead of the boat.

The *OED* provides two citations that, taken together, may answer both questions. The first citation is simply a quotation from another dictionary, *The Sailor's Word-Book*, which was compiled by Admiral William Henry Smith and published a couple of years after his death, in 1867. He defines *push* as "to move a vessel by poles." The *OED* follows that definition with another—it is not clear whether it is from the same source or not: *to push* (intransitive)—"to sit abaft an oar and propel the boat with forward strokes: as, to push down a stream." The first of these definitions describes the means of propulsion—poling. But the second comes into play as well, firstly because a hunter pushing the grass is always in fact using an oar, not a pole; and secondly because it is an intransitive use of the verb: "as, to push down a stream." A rower who sits astern of the oars, facing forward, propels the boat by pushing, rather than by pulling, the oars through the water. In practice, that means he is going with the current ("down a stream"—not up it), or that there is no current, and it means that being able to look ahead is more important to him than speed. So with the gunner in the gunning float.

And, finally, the oldest floats, built before the outboard era, frequently had a rowing seat and oarlocks on them. They were probably often *pushed*—rowed with the guide or hunter facing forward, to keep a lookout for ducks on the water or in the air ahead of him, rather than with the rower facing aft and pulling on the oars. The introduction of outboards changed all that, but the intransitive use of *push*, in relation to oar-powered propulsion, hung around.

6. *Peganaw, peganeau, peganau* (noun). I cannot find that this word has ever been written down or defined, and I have no notion of its origin—Abenaki? French? It is not currently in use around the Bay, but John Edgecomb, Ronnie Burrell, and Buster Prout have all told me the same thing—it was a term used to describe a small sturgeon. "Small" seems to mean not more than about four feet long, which might suggest that the word was another name for the short-nosed sturgeon. But this is not clear—Buster and Ronnie thought it likely that it was used for any sturgeon that was that size, whether a short-nose or an immature Atlantic. To sturgeon fishermen, the important distinction would have been size, not species, and they may well have considered a mature Atlantic to be a sturgeon, and everything else a mere peganaw (*sic?*).

W HEN I SAT IN DRUCKENMILLER HALL listening to hunters, students, and a couple of professors palaver about ducks, it set me thinking about how they talked, and about language in general. It was not exclusively a matter of vocabulary but also of cadence, pronunciation, and of assumptions. The hunters were of course older than the students, and they were also what used to be called "men of their hands"—men of exceptional manual skill and practical ability. Buster was a house painter, Ronnie a woodcutter, Adelbert a well driller, and all of them were good at making things—gunning floats, oars, houses—and at fixing things. They tended to think specifically and concretely, and to ground their generalizations in particular things they had seen at particular times in particular places around the Bay.

The students came at things through ideas and systems

of nomenclature—there were, after all, professors in the room who had trained them to do exactly that. They wanted to arrive at explanations that might, for example, connect the history of sedimentation and pollution in the Bay to its vegetation to its attractiveness to some species of waterfowl and not to others.

You can think of language by analogy to water and say that it is good to the extent that it is transparently and utterly clear, and that we know its goodness more by the absence of any identifying characteristics such as color, odor, flavor, opacity than by the presence of them. Good water looks, smells, and tastes like good water, wherever it comes from—that is, you can see right through it, can't smell it, and can't taste it.

Or you can think of language by analogy to wine, as having body and bouquet; having, at its best, subtle indicators of its age, of the variety or varieties of grape that it contains, and of where they were grown. The most highly prized vintages are frequently from a very restricted area—a region, sub-region, or even a particular vineyard.

In practice, language is a mixture of wine and water—to some degree diluted or adulterated, depending on how you look at it. The botanist who speaks of wild rice as *Zizania*

aquatica achieves a great precision (provided, that is, that she is speaking to other botanists) and also implies a clinical neutrality toward the plant: it exists in relation to a system of binomial nomenclature, but not in relation to herself. The hunter who refers to it as *the grass* will be misunderstood by everyone who is not a hunter—insofar as I know, by everyone who is not a hunter who hunts on the Bay. But, once you understand it, the word, like a good wine, invites you to linger over it, think about its provenance and its associations and connotations. And, although I cannot be sure about this, I have the impression that when a hunter refers to the tall plants that grow on the tide flats, he pronounces *grass* slightly differently than he does when he refers to the stuff that grows in his lawn. The vowel is a bit more open, and held for a nanosecond longer. The same is true when he is speaking of *birds* and not referring just to anything that has feathers and flies, but exclusively to ducks—as, for example, the hunter at the Bowdoinham town landing did, when he said there was a PAH-s'l of *birds* out there. There's a sense that the word is being savored for a moment—*italicized*, so to speak— and that a world lies solidly behind it. When a word is treated that way, you feel that there is, or can be, an intimate, solid relation between earth's daughters and heaven's sons.

Buster Prout: the craftsman and the craft

Intelligent Design

THE GUNNING FLOAT IS A PREDATORY SPECIES that appears on the Bay around the beginning of October, quickly establishing itself as the dominant watercraft. Three weeks later, they disappear, then they reappear two or three weeks after that, although in smaller numbers. Their range is almost entirely confined to Merrymeeting Bay. Most roost along its shoreline at night, and, when the coves ice over, migrate inland a few miles to hibernate in barns, garages, or sheds. Stocking programs have established token populations in other watersheds and even in other regions of the country, but they cannot properly be said to be indigenous to those places. Their reproductive rate is extremely low, and they are not known to breed outside of our area. They are, however, long-lived, in part, no doubt, because they are dormant for nine or ten months of the year.

Strictly speaking, they probably should be considered as a breed, one that has adaptively evolved to the circumstances of a highly distinctive environment, rather than as a separate species. Closely related boats are found from the Maritime Provinces to Barnegat Bay, New Jersey; the archeological and historical record, to say nothing of common sense, argues that the Merrymeeting Bay float evolved from them, rather than they from it.

The mists of time obscure the earliest development of this highly distinctive seasonal resident of the Bay. As a general rule, we may postulate that when waterfowl—its exclusive prey—existed in such staggering abundance that they were easily taken, predatory watercraft were not highly specialized—canoes, dugouts, punts, prams, and other such small, manually propelled, multipurpose, shallow-draft vessels would have sufficed. The evolution of the gunning float, whether in Merrymeeting Bay or elsewhere, was driven by the decrease in the overall numbers of waterfowl, and by the increase in the wariness of the individual duck or goose. A related, and crucially important, influence was the evolution of sport hunting in general, and especially of the emergence of the duck-hunting guide as an adjunct to it. In order to survive, the guides needed to accommodate themselves and their clients comfortably, and to give their clients a good chance of success. Competition among guides would at first have accelerated the evolutionary development of the float as less well-adapted and less efficient specimens were eliminated from the gene pool. In time, the same competition would have led them to perpetuate a single, maximally efficient design—a distinct breed. The evolutionary history of the gunning float has thus existed in dynamic symbiosis with that of the duck-hunting guide, to such an extent that the guide has typically been directly involved with the conception and reproduction of the float. Barring some almost unimaginable reversal of current trends, the Merrymeeting Bay duck-hunting guide will die out as a species within a generation. We cannot predict whether the gunning float in its current form will survive this; evidence of morphological change already exists, although we cannot at this point conclude that it foretells the evolutionary future.

That's how I am tempted to describe them, because they belong so naturally to the Bay and because, like a bird, fish, reptile, or mammal, each one closely resembles other members of its species without being a mass-produced replication of them; and because their evolution has been driven by a variety of intraspecific and environmental circumstances, and so casts some light on those circumstances.

I KNOW OF ONLY TWO ACCOUNTS of Maine gunning floats. One, published in *Down East* magazine in November 1966, describes Jim Whitney, a guide, decoy-maker, and gunning float builder, who was the son of a guide, decoy maker, and gunning-float builder. Father and son were from down around Falmouth, and so not directly relevant to Merrymeeting Bay, but they and their floats offer analogies and differences, both instructive, to the Merrymeeting builders and their floats. By the time *Down East* got to him, the younger Whitney was seventy-five years old and reckoned that over the course of his career he had turned out over five hundred gunning floats, all based on his father's design and all built in Falmouth, in his father's original shop. As far as I have ever heard, no builder around the Bay produced boats at anything like this rate—ten a year, assuming that Whitney went at it for a full fifty years of his life. He obviously had a big market—too big to be strictly local—and it probably included few, if any, guides.

One look at the photographs in *Down East* makes it clear that Whitney floats were primarily intended for salt water. That meant they could have been used in bays and estuaries anywhere from Nova Scotia to Long Island Sound and even points south of there. They differ from the floats around the Bay in something of the way that a sea duck—an eider or scoter—differs from a puddle duck—a black, mallard, or teal. That is, the Whitney float is chunkier, less graceful, and rides more deeply in the water. It has a V bottom instead of a rounded one, and a small keel runs the length of it. It would have been slower and less maneuverable than its Merrymeeting cousin, but better able to hold its course in a cross wind, and exceptionally stable in rough water. The fore-deck separating the cockpit from the bow is relatively more extensive, or, to put it the other way, the cockpit is relatively smaller. The coaming around the cockpit is low.

The floats illustrated in the article are built for a single gunner, and so would have been owner-operated, with no place for a guide. That in itself is interesting—there were plenty of ducks down along the coast, but they were not concentrated in the way that they were in Merrymeeting Bay, and so coastal communities lacked the culture of guides and hunting camps that grew up around the Bay, and that necessitated a boat that would accommodate two people. (I have seen one or two one-man floats that were made around the Bay—they were basically smaller versions of the standard Bay float—but they never seem to have been produced in any numbers.)

If Whitney was building the same basic boat that his father built, then we can assume that the design originated at least a century ago. In 1966 it had oarlocks, as well as a sculling port, but did not have a transom suitable for even the smallest of outboard motors. Unless they towed it behind a larger boat, the hunters who used it apparently hunted within a mile or so of the landing or mooring they set out from. They basically used it in two ways—to scull ducks in open water, or as a blind—with the hunter lying down inside and the decks covered with grass mats, the boat would look like a tiny mud flat.

The other account is in John Gardner's *Building Classic Small Craft* (Enlarged Edition, 1997). It provides a boat-builder's account of a Merrymeeting Bay gunning float built by Will Rittal of Richmond. Rittal built the float in 1975, but he was over ninety at the time, and the boat Gardner describes turned out to be his last. It was built on forms Rittal had used for all of his life as a boatbuilder, and that were not new when he acquired them. So its basic design would have been roughly contemporary with the Whitney float, and it seems to have made no concessions to modernity—for example, even in 1975, Rittal's boat still had a rowing seat and oarlocks, features I have never seen on any float in use on the Bay. Gardner describes Rittal's boat as, "probably as genuine a specimen of the type as has survived." If by "genuine," he means "old," he may or may not be right. But if he meant to imply that Rittal's boat closely resembles the Merrymeeting Bay float as it has existed for the past seventy-five years or so, then he is certainly wrong.

I do not know when the form currently prevalent evolved. My own boat, an example of it, was built by Buster Prout in 2000. It is essentially identical to the first float that Buster ever built, in 1960, and that he still uses. That one was built on the forms of Tom Wildes, and under his tutelage. Buster estimates that Wildes was at that time about eighty years old, and that the forms dated back to at least the 1930s. Buster—about nineteen years old at that time—had already gunned in one of Wildes's floats. He found it cramped—forty-two inches was its maximum width—and so widened it by half a foot. To preserve the sharply pointed bow that would allow it to move easily through the grass, he needed to lengthen it by a foot. Buster thinks that Wildes's

A quarter-scale model

float may have derived from ones built by a yet older-timer named Foggy Wilson—either that, or the Wilde float and the Wilson one shared a common ancestor. Buster suspects that his own float is typical in being somewhat larger than its progenitor. "A lot of those old-timers would just pretty much hunt one cove. They might go back and forth across the Abby or the Cathance or Eastern, but they didn't go up and down the big rivers the way we do today. And they didn't have outboards, so they didn't need room to lay 'em down inside when they got to sculling. We need a little more boat now."

You can get a better idea of what the Prout version of the Merrymeeting Bay gunning float looks like by consulting Heather's pictures than I can give you in print. But here, roughly speaking, is what we are talking about:

I. It is sixteen feet long and four feet wide, beamiest just aft of midships and tapering slightly from that point to the transom, which is forty inches wide. The bottom is rounded. The cockpit is defined by a coaming that is eight inches higher than the narrow deck between it and the gunwales. A thwart, necessary for structural rigidity, divides the cockpit into two compartments. The thwart, like the coamings, is made of half-inch-by-eight-inch pine. On the back side of it is a narrow shelf, a place for the hunter in the stern to put his shells. If you are a first-time passenger in my float, I will point out a feature of the float that is apparently not apparent to many people, namely that, *The #%*!^*ing thwart is not a*

An eighth-scale model

Installing steamed oak ribs

Rib installation complete

#%^&**ing seat!!!! Don't take it personally.

2. Seen from above, a Merrymeeting Bay float looks something like a square-sterned version of a seagoing kayak—one with an open cockpit. Its long, tapering bow chiefly accounts for this resemblance. From the same perspective, the Whitney float looks more like a square-sterned version of a whitewater kayak—which is to say, like a square-sterned watermelon seed.

3. Seen in profile, from the bow to a point three-quarters of the way back, the Merrymeeting float keeps its resemblance to a seagoing kayak—the keel line (there is no actual keel) is perfectly flat, parallel to the line of the gunwales, and the distance between the two is only about nine inches. You are looking at a boat that is designed to move through the water, not over it. But in its final four feet, the hull curves sleekly upward, evoking not a kayak but the stern of a schooner. It is hard to convey the grace of this. When afloat, with the motor removed and the boat properly trimmed, the bottom of the transom barely touches the water. Anyone who has ever tried to paddle a square-sterned canoe can appreciate the importance of this in reducing drag.

4. The port for the sculling oar is two inches in diameter. It is located four inches from the bottom of the transom and somewhat left of center. If there is a following wind, a bit of water may slop through the hole when you reach over

the stern to insert the oar into it. But when you stretch out to scull, you are shifting the weight far forward enough to lift the bottom of the transom above water level, and even a strong tailwind and a heavy chop cause no problem. In rough water and cold weather, you may, however, need to shift your psychological ballast around a bit before you can feel quite comfortable in operating a boat that has a two-inch hole that close to the waterline.

5. Because they are homemade, Merrymeeting Bay gunning floats are not officially rated either in terms of their carrying capacity or the maximum horsepower they can accommodate. Their floor plan basically limits them to two people. But if the two people wanted to carry the equivalent of a third, in the form of decoys, equipment, or a hefty Labrador retriever, they could do it safely. The horsepower is as much a matter of practicality as safety. The hull design does not allow the boat to plane—to skim across the surface—and this means that on my float, for example, much more than five horsepower would simply be wasted. I use a four-horse motor; Buster has a three, and three-horse motors are probably the commonest size. John Edgecomb tells me that the hunters around the Androscoggin mouth, who dealt with bigger water and bigger distances, traditionally favored somewhat bigger floats, and you see five- and six-horsepower motors in use there.

Because the boat rides low in the water and has narrow decks along the sides, it is virtually uncapsizable. It feels extremely steady, like a much larger boat. Heading into a short, steep chop on a rough day is, however, a wet, cold experience, particularly for the passenger, who gets the brunt of the spray coming in over the bow. And there comes a point when you do not risk it—the danger would be burying the nose of the boat in oncoming swells, taking on water in the cockpit, and so reducing buoyancy, therefore taking on more water from the next swell, and so forth. The hull of a gunning float in fact bears considerable resemblance to the hull of a submarine, but is not designed for subsurface operation.

6. Buster's floats, like all of the wooden floats that I have ever seen on the Bay, are strip-built and edge-nailed. The builder lays a sixteen-foot plank on a strongback. The plank is widest—about nine inches on my boat—where the finished boat will be widest, and its taper fore and aft matches that of the boat from stem to stern. Four feet from the stern, it is through-bolted to the strongback and a chock is placed under its end, to establish the upward lift of the stern. So the builder now has the bent backbone of the float. The transom and a rather complex prow piece, made of solid cedar, are attached at each end. The forms, which determine the overall shape of the hull, are spaced in between. The first strakes, strips of white pine, half an inch thick and an inch and a half wide at their widest, are attached to the backbone on

either side by nails running through them and into the edge of the bottom plank. In width, the taper of the strakes conforms to the taper of the bottom plank. Ensuing strakes are through-nailed and tapered in the same way. As the sides curve upward, each strake must be beveled along its edge to fit perfectly and along its entire length to the inboard strake to which it is attached. When the hull is complete, but not yet decked, the ribs—steamed oak, quarter-inch thick and one-and-a-half-inches wide—are forced into place, at one-foot intervals, and clinch-nailed. This is the only part of the job that requires two people, one to drive the nails and one to hold a clinching iron—usually something like the head of a maul—against the ribs to bend the nails as they come through. A boat built this way is built from the outside in, as though you were to build a house by starting with the clapboards and then attaching the studs to them. Carvel-planked boats are built from the inside out—first the ribs are bent into place over a form, and then the planking is nailed to them.

7. The finished hull, held together by hardware without benefit of epoxy or other glues, is as tight as a teakettle. But Buster is no purist. He has John Edgecomb fiberglass the outside of the hull, to protect the soft pine against the sharp-edged shell ice that you motor through late in the season, and to prevent shrinking during the boat's long season of hibernation.

THE RITTAL BOAT'S HULL DESIGN differed from what is now the standard design in important respects. Looked at from above, it tapered gradually and evenly from its beamiest point toward the bow and toward the stern, making the bow compartment much wider and more spacious. The forward end of the boat was thus far less elongated than in the floats currently in use. And the Rittal boat did not have the dramatically uplifted schooner stern that I have described. It had a shallow keel that ran the length of the bottom. The keel was no more than an inch deep for almost the entire length of the boat, and perhaps two inches deep at the transom, because the stern turned very slightly upward. This design produced a boat that sat lightly on the water. When rowed, the long, flat keel-line gave it a longer glide between strokes—that would have been, I believe, its chief advantage over the modern design, even if the modern design were equipped with oarlocks and a rowing seat.

The Rittal float was carvel-built. To my mind, it represents a sort of paleogunning float, an intermediate stage of the species' evolution away from a conventional rowboat or skiff. From all that one reads and garners by listening to the old hunters who are also the oral historians of hunting on the Bay, Rittal's boat would have served admirably through about the 1920s. A guide or hunter could have gotten to where he was going more quickly and easily than in a boat like mine, and have had a bit more leg and elbow room once he got there. And ducks were so numerous that the higher profile of his boat would not have mattered. But outboard motors reduced the Rittal's margin of advantage, and the diminishing numbers and growing sophistication of the ducks made its disadvantages more telling. The specimen that Gardner based his account on was used by a Connecticut hunter in Long Island Sound; Rittal's boat, like Whitney's, may have been better suited for a wider range of habitats, but it was less well suited to the Bay itself.

Buster had seen a few of the Rittal boats and had known Will Rittal himself. I asked him his opinion of the design. Buster does not like to criticize people, or say things about them that he would not be willing to say to them, and so he hedged a little. In his book, John Gardner was freer in his opinions:

> It appears that some of the later floats [than Rittal's] were strip planked, perhaps by builders who lacked the confidence and skill for carvel planking. Because of the shape of the hull, which tapers toward the bow, strip planking would present some problems as well. I should want to reserve judgment on strip-built boats until I had a chance to inspect them. Nevertheless, to me strip planking suggests decadence.

Set against Buster's unwillingness to speak unkindly was his lifelong commitment to the art and craft of building gunning floats, which carries with it a lifelong habit of looking carefully at every one he sees. When I pressed him further on the subject of the Rittal float, he delivered his judgement reluctantly, with the reserved gravity and deliberation that are typical of him: "Old man Will's boats were pretty rough, I thought. What you'd call *gaumy*, but that's just in my opinion." Certainly Gardner's peremptory judgment that the tapered bow would present a greater challenge to strip planking than to carvel planking is not borne out by the evidence: the taper is much more dramatic in Buster's boat than in Rittal's. Without knowing anything about Gardner, or about boatbuilding, I would defy him to walk into Buster Prout's shop, observe him at work, examine the finished product, and conclude that the boat was suggestive of decadence, and of a lack of confidence and skill on the part of the boatbuilder.

I like everything about the Prout float. I like the fact that it, like a wood-canvas canoe, is ribbed and planked with pieces of wood so slender that you could easily break any of them over your knee, and yet for all its delicacy and lightness of construction is a tough, capable boat. Those things suit it to the birds that are its quarry. I like the whole experience of sculling, which I will try to describe in just a minute. I like its cozy minimalism, which encourages you to think of all the things you can do without when your purpose is duck hunting. And I like the steady feel of it under power, and its slippery stealth in the grass.

But I believe that this classic boat will probably continue to evolve, and that its evolution will be, ironically enough, back in the direction of the Rittal float. John Edgecomb is the case in point. He's a decade younger than Buster, and no less accomplished. He told me how, during World War II, his grandfather had two sons—John's father and his uncle—overseas and in harm's way. Like so many civilians, he felt the need to do something helpful, for the good of the troops and also to occupy his mind. Rather than planting a victory garden or collecting scrap metal, he began building a gunning float, as his contribution to the war effort or as a kind of prayer. It worked on both counts—we won the war, and his boys came home. John used those same molds to build his first gunning float, in the traditional way.

He has continued to build: floats, his house, a greenhouse, a workshop, a pond—he perhaps learned from his grandfather that building things and building them right keeps harm away. And, unlike Buster, he keeps experimenting. He field-tests his new designs for a few years, then sells them and incorporates what he has learned into his next design. His current float is three years old. Like the Rittal, it has a flat keel-line, is beamy, and carries its beaminess up into the bow compartment. It is considerably deeper than Buster's

float. It has no sculling port, and it would be a penance to try to push it through the grass. John runs an eight-horse motor on it, which is big enough to lift it up and send it skimming across the Bay. It is, in other words, strictly for use as a mobile blind.

John's view is this: "You've got to cover a lot of water now, to find where the ducks are feeding. Not like in the old days, when you could set up about anywhere and count on the ducks coming to you. Not as many ducks, not as much competition for food, so they travel together in big flocks. You can go to four or five coves and not see a bird, then go to the sixth and there's a thousand of 'em." John, God knows, isn't lazy, and he's an accomplished sculler. But he has made up his mind—the effective way to hunt is to hunt over decoys; the features that made the traditional float an optimal sculling boat made it a somewhat cramped blind, and, when it came to covering a lot of water in a hurry, a decidedly suboptimal motor boat, and so he has eliminated those features.

There are in fact very few hunters who scull on the Bay now. Most do what John does, although not as effectively. His boat is atypical at present, but possibly prototypical in the long run. And it is a design that would work well in many of the different environments in which ducks are hunted. If I were an investor, I would invest my money in his design. It has growth potential, nationally and locally, and every detail of it is well thought-out. If you know how to operate any kind of boat, you will know how to operate it—no specialized training is required.

But if duck hunting were done on a strictly practical basis, it wouldn't be done at all. Aesthetic preferences, which may or may not have philosophic underpinnings, play a part in it. The Prout boat pleases me as much as anything I have ever owned, and I have tried to learn to use it as it was meant to be used.

THE OLD-TIMERS WHO GREW UP GUIDING—Linwood Rideout, Ronnie, Buster, Adelbert—like to talk about how they hunted, starting in the thirties or forties or fifties, and continuing up into the seventies. Linwood goes all the way back to the live-decoy era: "We usually carried three or four. They just had a short line on one leg with a snap on it, and you'd clip 'em all to a long trawl line. Sometimes we'd hold one hen back by the boat. She'd want to get out there with the others, and set up an awful quacking. At least some would. You learned which ducks were talkative, and tried to get at least one of them for yourself and your sport." An Englishman who spent a couple of weeks duck hunting with Linwood sent him a *flyer* when he got back to England, as a token of appreciation. She'd be released from the boat when a flock was in sight, fly out to them, then fly back to the boat, quacking away. "A traitor to her kind," Linwood called

Completed hull, as yet undecked. Note the cedar bow piece.

her, and he used her with great success until, inevitably, a hunter got confused and killed the double agent by mistake. Roasting her was unthinkable—she was buried with full military honors.

There were hunting camps around the Bay—sometimes bunkhouses, sometimes one-room cabins, like the ones still out on Pleasant Point. Hunters might come up for only a weekend, but a lot of them tried to make at least a week of it. Each camp had a mess hall, where everybody ate, as in the traditional sporting camps that still exist up in the North Woods. Each had its own stable of guides. Late in the summer, before the season opened, some of them took their scythes down to the Bay and did a bit of landscaping in the grass—mowing out a little pond, no bigger than a tennis court, then cutting a channel. The channel would come out of the pond and dogleg sharply before going on into shore, so that a duck sitting in the pond couldn't see down it. A diagrammatic drawing of it would look like a diagrammatic drawing of a shad weir—sometimes several smaller ponds, each with its own private channel, sometimes a bigger one, with several boat paths converging on it. It could be Buster or Linwood or Ronnie describing how it worked:

Sometimes, there at the foot of Swan Island, with a coming tide, half a dozen of us would put decoys into one opening, then pull on into the bank, get out, stretch our legs, set, and talk. Leave the sports in the boats, or they might come join us. With all our decoys in one spot, we weren't in competition with each other. If a single or a few teal set into them, we'd just leave 'em be—there'd be more along soon. And when there were half a dozen or a dozen or so ducks out there, we'd slip back to our floats.

We took turns—one guide sculling his sport out. The next boat to his right could go out, too, but that one had to keep behind, maybe get a pass shot after the flush. Next time, that boat would go out first, and the one to its right would follow. Everybody else just sat back on the shore and watched. Some sports didn't want their guide to shoot, and some did. Course you liked it better when he let you shoot—even if your sport couldn't hit the backside of a barn, you'd still get two limits of ducks that way. Sometimes, it got to where you'd try to shoot the bird he was shooting at, so you could tell him he hit it.

And then some days, maybe when it was high water in the middle of the day, I might take my sport out onto the Bay early, and we'd see what he could do there, and then when the tide started in good, we'd scull up the Abby, have lunch with us, make a day of it. Get up to the millpond, up there at the head of tide, and we might set out the decoys there while we had lunch. But it was mostly jump shooting, and it could be good, as long as there wasn't somebody going up there just ahead of us. It was a nice change of pace, and a lot of the hunters I took up there liked it.

Ronnie tell you about that blind man he took out? Lost both his eyes in France, in the war. Before the war he used to come up here all the time—good shot, too; crack shot, in fact, and he loved his hunting. He come back from the war and he told Ronnie they were going to go out, scull off the foot of the Island, just like always. Said he'd be able to tell where to

shoot from the noise the birds made getting up. And from what I under-
stand, he did get a few—Ronnie'd wait till a whole gang of birds had set-
tled in, maybe a hundred or more. Then he'd slip out there extra careful, get
close, and clap his hands. They'd all jump at once, and that guy would shoot
at the sound. Course I expect Ronnie shot just when he did sometimes, and
in a big flock like that, Ronnie'd stand a pretty good chance of knocking
down a couple of birds with one shot. Fella finally quit duck hunting and
moved south and took up that blind golf they play down there. I don't
know how that works, but he got serious about it and good at it, too—or
so he said. It sounded sad to me.

But you got all kinds. Ronnie used to take out a doctor from
Brunswick every year. Talk your ear off, then he'd stop, and you might
make a remark or two yourself, while you were watching for birds. Then
you'd turn, and there he'd be, head back, mouth hanging open, fast asleep.
Once Ronnie sculled him toward a bunch of geese they saw pitch down in
the Kennebec. It was way out, and the geese kept edging away when they'd
be about to get in range, and it was quite some time before they finally got
up in good range and Ronnie said, "All right—let 'em have it." Nothin'
happened—Doc was fast asleep. It was like he had two speeds, sleeping
and talking, but he was a nice, nice guy. Maybe not the man you'd go to to
get your appendix out, though.

THE FIRST TIME I MET BUSTER PROUT was in his shop, in
the winter of 1999–2000. For the previous thirty years, I
duck hunted from a canoe—most commonly an old eight-
een-foot Old Town wood-canvas one. It was an easy way to
hunt, and fairly effective during the first two weeks of the
first season, before the rice began to thin out and fall down. I
did best at low tide and at first light, which further reduced
my hunting time on the Bay. Later in the season, I did some
hunting in other places, usually in small inlets along the
coast, where I could put out decoys and hide myself on the
bank. Wherever I hunted, I seldom shot from the canoe
itself—it was just the means to get me where I was going and
to retrieve what I had shot. I was a nonspecialist in hunting
as in all other things, and was inclined to think of that as a
virtue. Canoes do not require you to fool with boat trailers
or outboard motors, and you can get them in and out of the
water where there are no formal landings. That simplicity was
important to me.

So I did not walk into Buster's shop with any idea of
investing in a specialized duck-hunting boat, or becoming a
more serious kind of duck hunter. I had been asked to get a
group of old hunters around the Bay together, to talk to the
Friends of Merrymeeting Bay. I'd spoken first to Linwood
Rideout, whom I knew, and thus knew to be the dean of the
Merrymeeting hunters, and he told me to talk to Buster, who
lived just down the road from him. I went there and don't
remember much about our discussion except that Buster was
willing to participate if the others were, and that, before I
left, he asked if I'd like to see the float he was working on.
We walked through a small garage that was full of odds and

ends—decoys, cans of paint, an old wood-canvas canoe, tools, ladders, a tattered and spattered painter's tarp spread out over something, a goodly collection of deer antlers mounted on one wall—and into the shop behind it. There was a box stove in the middle, some lumber neatly spaced and racked for drying on overhead shelves, decoys—mostly black duck, but some whistlers—lining one wall, and a work bench along the opposite wall. In the middle, upright on sawhorses, was a gunning float that he'd just begun to work on. I asked him about it; rather than explain, he took me back out into the garage, and together we lifted up the painter's tarp I had noticed. Beneath it was a new-built gunning float. It was intended for a Massachusetts hunter who came up every fall to hunt the Bay.

I don't think of myself as an impulse buyer, and I spent a week dutifully trying to argue myself out of what I already knew I was going to do, then called Buster and asked him if the float under construction was bespoke. He said it wasn't yet, I said it was now, and that was that. Through the rest of the winter, I dropped by from time to time to watch it take shape.

When the boat was finished, but still unpainted, it looked like something that belonged in a museum or a shrine—certainly not like something to be put into muddy water, or stepped into and out of by men wearing muddy boots, or by muddy dogs with muddy paws, or dragged across mud flats, or, in honor of its environment, painted the color of mud. In 1753 William Hogarth theorized that there is something called the "line of beauty" that underlies our whole notion of what is and isn't beautiful. It is a "constantly flowing and delicately varying" line that is "both bent and twisted." We prefer it because we subconsciously recognize it as being fundamentally anatomical, evident in the slight curvature and spiral of the thighbone, or the skeinlike sag and twist of muscle, or the fluid contours of the body as a whole. Looked at from any angle, that is what the unpainted float revealed. I suppose that that is not surprising— boats are, in the strictest sense, *streamlined*—smoothly continuous, narrow at the forward end, bellying outward toward the middle, and rounding off astern. Their shape is defined by the same logic that shapes a sandbar between two runnels of moving water. But every element of this boat—a single strake running from stem to stern, the curved silhouette of the transom, or of the skeg beneath the stern—reinforced its effect. Looking at it made you want to run your hand over it. Even the duckboards that provide a dry and level platform for the man in the stern matched the taper from transom to midships, and so did every slat in them.

It was May by the time the last coat of paint had dried. Buster went out with me in the boat to demonstrate sculling. I watched him do it for awhile. He sat sideways, his back propped against the coaming, and pushed and pulled the oar, wagging it back and forth, but with a rolling motion of the wrists. When he did this rapidly, the power of the to-and-fro thrust of the oar made the boat rock jerkily from side to side, but when he slowed down, the boat steadied, and crept ahead as though it were self-propelled. I tried my hand at it that day, and found that my hand had a lot to learn. I took the boat out a good many times during the summer, and finally muscle memory took over—I no longer needed to think about what I was doing, and began doing it pretty well.

A sculling oar is eight feet long. The blade is a little over three feet long, straight-sided, square-ended, and narrow— about four and three-quarter inches wide. It is flat on one side, and convex on the other. A leather sleeve, about a foot long, is usually wrapped around the shaft of the oar, about eighteen inches above the blade. It covers the section of the shaft that fits inside the port, saves wear and tear on the oar, and prevents any rattling. You usually gob a bit of Vaseline on it before sculling, to reduce friction. The flat side of the oar is its working surface; the convex side allows you to flip the oar over easily, at the end of the stroke. Beneath the water, the blade works in a horizontal figure-eight pattern, like a long, two-bladed, and shallowly pitched propeller.

Do this:

1. Hold your hands chest high and in front of you, palms down, and forefingers touching. Then bend your fingers downward. You are now gripping the shaft of the oar. It is not perfectly horizontal, so your right hand should be slightly higher than your left.

2. Cock your wrists up, and draw your hands in towards you, almost to your chest.

3. Rotate your wrists downward, and push your hands away from you, until your elbows are almost straight.

4. Repeat step two, then step three, and so forth, until the motion becomes fluid and continuous. You will find that your hands, like the other end of the oar, are moving in a shallow, horizontal figure-eight movement. Each rotation of your wrists turns the flat face of the oar over, so that you are always pushing it or pulling it against the water.

This strange means of locomotion, so unlike traditional rowing or paddling, determines the shape, size, and profile of a gunning float. You can do it sitting on the bottom of the boat. When you are actually approaching birds, you lie down flat, your neck and shoulders resting on a little prop-board built into the angle between the transom and the side of the cockpit. This barely enables you to peek over the front deck of the boat. From the perspective of the duck, your hands, busily in motion, are entirely invisible, and so is the oar. The duck sees only the low, narrow wedge of the bow. You see the duck by lifting your head slightly and very cautiously. In your means of propulsion and the slow, low-profile stealth of your stalk, you resemble an alligator or crocodile, flexing its tail gently and slowly, creating no wake, only its eyes and the bump of its snout visible. If your eyes, like its, protruded from the top of your head, it would save you considerable stiffness of neck and soreness of back.

In the first year I owned the float, and in the years since then, I have taken so much pleasure in sculling that it has rather reduced my overall effectiveness as a hunter. The sculler's map of the Bay is a map of creeks, guzzles, and indented shores, and it changes from tide to tide. You need eighteen inches of water, a channel that is not less than five feet wide, and that has enough current to have little or no vegetation growing in it—even a small amount of grass catches the oar. You move slowly until you see something, then you slide down on your spine and move more slowly. Herons do not lift their heads or cease their fishing as you approach them. Once a solitary sandpiper fluttered a few inches above the front deck of the float, and would have landed if it had not seen the movement of my hands. Another time, I studied a mat of rice stems six feet off to the side of the boat for several seconds before I understood that what made it look slightly odd was a Wilson's snipe, crouched low and studying me, its inky-black and shining droplet of an eye the one thing that betrayed it as something alive. Keeping still, and keeping your silhouette lower than what is around you, gives you a sort of invisibility, or at least makes you into something of a puzzle. That was true of me when I looked at the snipe, and true

of the snipe when it looked at me.

Up the Muddy River, I sculled by a Cooper's hawk—a jumpy, high-strung bird—perched on a snag, just above the water. It was only chance that I saw him, and could go into full stealth mode and watch him as I sculled past. He cocked his head and fidgeted, unsure whether to fly or not to fly until I was almost by him, and the movement of the oar between the transom and the water alarmed him. Beaver too—the upper Cathance is crawling with them, and I've had one swim across in front of me, ten feet from the bow, heave himself out onto the bank, and laboriously hump his way across a mud flat, his tail flopping along behind him, so that he looked and sounded like a car crawling along on a flat tire. More commonly, you excite their suspicions—they are suspicious by nature, and also bad-tempered, self-righteous, and somewhat nearsighted paragons of the work ethic, all drudgery and begrudgery, as far as I can see—and they swim toward the float, raise their heads, fix you with a pig-eyed glare, flex their tails, and deliver a mighty *whap* on the water, apparently expecting that to vaporize you on the spot. When it doesn't, they may accompany you for some time, repeating the experiment. Muskrats, on the other hand, are timid, and quick to arch up their backs and slide beneath the surface. But if you are quiet and keep still, they will swim right alongside. Their forelegs are tucked in against their chests, and their vertically flattened tails move from side to side, in the manner of a sculling oar. If Ovid had lived on the Bay, he would no doubt have concocted a myth about how a duck hunter, in the course of some sort of bad encounter with the gods, was metamorphosed into a muskrat.

But for all of this, you are after ducks, and see so much in part because you are so attentive to anything that looks slightly odd against the bank or at the edge of the grass, or to any slight movement back in the grass, or to even the faintest quiver of a ripple from a small point of land or at a bend in a creek. Your own horizons are close and narrow, bounded by a twisting guzzle or the shoreline that you hug as closely as you can, sometimes sculling under branches that hang low over the water, requiring you to lie flat as you glide beneath them. You learn the concealment value of shadow—even bright drake mallards seem to fade into it and become monochrome, part of a shifting pattern of partially obstructed light, wholly obstructed light, and reflected light that plays against the bank. What conceals them conceals you, and if you are in shadow and they are in sunlight, you have a degree of advantage. But if the sun is behind you, so that you are coming out of it toward them, and they are looking into the dazzling path of its reflection, that is a help. Do peregrines avail themselves of this, and hurtle down out of the sun whenever they can?

So the boat in many ways has made the Bay a new place for me, and given me some idea of how it must appear to a swimming black duck or teal, putting me closer to the things they feed on and making me more precisely aware of the hourly changes within the intertidal zone. It has also made me much more aware than previously of my own limitations as a hunter, or, to put it the other way, how extraordinarily skillful and knowing the real Bay hunters are. Buster, as far as I can see, never sculls along the edge of a cove that does not hold ducks, never motors past one that does, and never puts out decoys and sits for more than half an hour before customers begin to appear. I don't worry about it—anything that is truly worth doing is even worth doing quite badly, because anything that is worth doing is to some degree an end in itself. You don't do it with that rationalization in your mind, however; it wouldn't be worth doing if you did.

Decoys in Buster's shop, few with their original heads

The Wild Common

In MOST OF THIS COUNTRY, freshwater duck hunting is an expensive sport. That was true even in my boyhood, and it is truer now. Flyways channel ducks along routes—the Atlantic and Pacific Coasts, the Mississippi, the eastern slope of the Rockies—that offer them an abundance of shallow water habitat: swamps, marshes, boggy ponds, potholes. Agriculture, logging, urbanization, residential development, navigational improvements, disease control—more or less every priority of our civilization and our economy—have tended toward the alteration or elimination of this terrain, so little of which was of direct, obvious utility. And so the ducks have been funneled and concentrated into fewer and fewer places. By the late-nineteenth century, wealthy sportsmen—sometimes individually, often incorporated into clubs—began buying or leasing prime duck habitat. Elsewhere, landowners adjacent to such habitat set up commercial operations, complete with guides, blinds, boats, and so forth, effectively monopolizing the hunting and turning a landscape into a recreational commodity, like a downhill-skiing operation.

Imagine yourself seventy or eighty years ago, living in Bowdoinham and owning a good deal of Bay frontage out on

Center Point. The farming isn't prosperous, commercial fishing has died out, and cash is hard to come by. It makes sense for you to find a way to capitalize on the duck hunting—prime duck marshes lie at your doorstep; local hunters walk down to them across your fields or through your woods. To begin with you rent out spare rooms in your farmhouse, hire some of the local duck hunters to serve as guides, using their own boats, and advertise by local word of mouth. Word spreads, business picks up, and you decide to expand. You put up some rustic accommodations, hire more guides, get the ones who have the time and skill to build some extra boats and sell them to you so that you can start hiring promising boys, who don't yet own boats of their own, but know the Bay pretty well. You now have enough of an operation to advertise in the Boston papers.

Things flourish, but you look to make them still better. You can promise your clients fine shooting, and you can absolutely guarantee them that the shooting will be within a few hundred feet of the place where they spend the night, so that they won't have to get up at an ungodly hour and go a long way by boat in the freezing dark in order to be in place and ready for business when daylight comes. But what you cannot promise them is exclusive access to that shooting, and that, after all, is what people are willing to pay the most for—the promise of exclusivity, whether it is in a duck marsh, a country club, a neighborhood, an educational institution,

or the Great Hereafter. You control access to the hunting from the land, but nobody controls access to it from the water. Your rights as a property owner stop at the high-tide line. The big, duck-rich marsh—the grass—is in the public domain, open to every Tom, Dick, and Harry who owns some kind of boat, some kind of gun, and a hunting license.

Knowing something about the history of land use in this country, you know that this kind of limitation on the rights of property owners—which is to say, this kind of affirmation of the rights of the general public—can be circumvented or simply ignored in practice. It was, after all, illegal to build dams across the Androscoggin in the early days of the young republic—the shad and salmon had the law squarely on their side when it came to riparian and navigational rights, and a fat lot of good it did them. So you scratch your head and think about life's great question, which is (let's be blunt about it) *how, without actually breaking the law, can I make more money?* Well, if you can eliminate, or at least reduce, your dependence on guides, that'll help—you'd no longer have to share your profits with them, maybe just hire one or two now and again. If you can figure out a way to monopolize the hunting on, let's say, Bluff Head Cove, which happens to lie out in front of your property, where you already have your sporting camps operating, then you can control how many people hunt there, which will surely improve the shooting, and allow you to attract a swankier clientele—people not rich enough to belong to one of the exclusive duck-hunting clubs further south, but rich enough to pay extra for a week or so of enjoying the illusion that they do.

So here is what you do. You groom the grass as usual, late in the summer—mow out openings in it to create small ponds, and mow little channels from in front of your camps out to them. Then, at the edge of each pond, you drive two stakes, a boat-length apart, deep into the mud. You tie a boat—any kind of old rowboat, flat-bottomed oversized pram, or undersized scow of a thing—between the two stakes in a way that allows it to move up and down with the tides, and you disguise it, using chicken wire or an old shad net or something like that, and weaving the mown rice stems into it. Out in front, in the little pond, you lay down a trawl line—a length of cord, weighted heavily at both ends, and with three or four lighter, buoyed lines attached to it. You mow out your ponds and stake out your boat blinds so that they are far enough apart to be out of shotgun range of each other, but not so far apart that there is really room for another hunter to come in and set out his decoys between them. You have not laid legal claim to the marsh or denied other hunters the right to hunt there. You have only moored some boats in it, and that breaks no law.

When the hunting season comes, your rules for visiting sportsmen are simple. Two hunters per blind. Each pair of hunters has a small, flat-bottomed boat, which they paddle out to the blind assigned to them for that day. They carry three or four live ducks with them, plus some wooden decoys. When they get to the blind—assuming they are even minimally competent, they will not need a guide for this— they clip the live decoys to the trawl line, put out a few wooden decoys around them, and get into the blind. They stay there—they do not hunt anywhere else. When they kill a duck, they paddle out in the small boat to get it. They are close to the lodge—if they want to paddle back to it for lunch or a nap, they can.

Let us imagine that you do this, and it works as well as you hope. Other camps around the Bay—the ones that are advantageously located—are going to imitate you. Soon, all of the best hunting will be effectively controlled by these camps. Guides and local hunters will suffer, because there are fewer and fewer good marshes for them to hunt in. Given the usual operations of a free-market economy, the larger and more efficient operations will tend to take over the smaller ones, and eventually duck hunting on Merrymeeting Bay will be controlled by a few big interests.

This is what did and did not happen around the Bay. That is, a smart operator devised and put into operation the system I have described—I promise you that I'm not nearly smart enough to have dreamed it up myself. This was a man named Darton, who owned a lot of land out on Center Point, including the frontage on Bluff Head Cove. It worked well. He undertook to expand his operation up to the Big Flats, at the mouth of the Eastern River, where he also had some property. Here he encountered resistance—the first and only blind he put up there one fine, late summer day vanished overnight. This could have been only a temporary setback. But he was running into a culture of guides, local hunters, and people whose families had lived out of the Bay, in one way or another, for generations, and who had seen its fisheries decline and fail, and who saw its ducks as perhaps its last significant economic resource. They lobbied Augusta and, lo and behold, Augusta acted.

A very simple law was passed—it was made illegal to erect any kind of permanent blind on Merrymeeting Bay, or even to leave out a spread of decoys overnight. And so the Bay has remained part of the public domain. Sporting camps continued to thrive along its shores, but none of them could monopolize the marshes. Among other things, this ensured that the Merrymeeting Bay guides, if they were to succeed, had to be men who knew a lot about the Bay, and who were skilled in the handling of a gunning float. Indeed, the law that passed in Augusta probably preserved the gunning float as a navigational indigene of Sagadahoc County, which is reason enough to be grateful to it. And it also preserved duck hunting as an ordinary amenity of local life, something that you could do if you had a hunting license and owned a gun and some kind of boat, or even a pair of hip boots.

It WAS VERY DIFFERENT WHERE I GREW UP, in a town that was somewhat closer to the ocean as the crow flew, but about twice as far upriver from it as Bowdoinham is. The primary hunting grounds were downriver, in the rice fields. During the second half of the eighteenth century, the original terrain of freshwater swamps, which were close enough to the ocean to be affected by the tides, but far enough from it to have no salt water intrusion, had been clear-cut and diked off from the rivers. Gates in the dikes controlled the flow of water in and out of the fields thus created, and, with the gates shut, canals and smaller drainage ditches could be dug in them, allowing them to be drained thoroughly, plowed, and sowed. Then the water was let back into the fields, flooding them to the proper depth for long-grain domestic rice, the seed imported originally from Madagascar, to grow there. Come harvest time, they were drained again.

The Civil War and the opening of more productive rice lands in Louisiana combined to kill off the industry, and the fields turned into marshes. These marshes, like the rice fields before them and the swamps before them, attracted ducks in great numbers, and they, and the old plantation houses along the banks, in turn attracted wealthy sportsmen. So the prime duck habitat of the South Carolina low country had not been accessible to ordinary hunters for a couple of centuries. My father and I hunted there by invitation only, and the invitations were not that frequent—two times a season, maybe three in a good year.

These marshes were predominantly saw grass. They, the canals, and the ditches provided good duck habitat, but were comparatively poor in feed. In my boyhood, if even one of the men who owned an old rice field "baited" it—put out corn or some other grain—the others were pretty much obliged to follow suit; otherwise, all the ducks would be drawn to his field. The practice was illegal and it was almost universal—a test of the owner's guilefulness or his political influence.

I loved the hunting itself, and those overgrown rice fields were strange, beautiful landscapes, the remnants of a past so radically unlike the present that it seemed vastly more remote than it was, and proportionately mysterious. But I didn't like all the baggage that went with it—didn't like the feeling that I was probably hunting illegally and was certainly hunting on what amounted to a private estate, maintained exclusively for that purpose. And there was something else I did not like, which was that a good many of the owners of the rice fields felt themselves entitled to all the ducks they could shoot, disregarding limits and even seasons in the same way they disregarded the laws against baiting. And, because duck hunting was so strictly a rich man's sport, a lot of ordinary hunters had no scruples about killing ducks whenever and however they could—poaching, in South Carolina as in Eng-

land, was a minor form of class warfare.

Maine was a remarkable contrast. You hunted ducks the way you hunted anything else—found a likely looking spot and, unless it was posted, went hunting. You didn't have to know anybody. It was do-it-yourself, trial-and-error, hit-or-miss, and it suited me fine. And there were a lot more ducks, especially black ducks, which were relatively uncommon in South Carolina, but were regarded there as they were in Maine—the prize quarry.

In hunting the way I hunted, I was in many ways reinventing the wheel, learning slowly and haphazardly things that people had figured out decades or centuries ago. I didn't mind—reinventing wheels is an underrated activity, a personal experience of generational history. I mostly hunted by myself, in order to waste nobody's time but my own, and to leave myself free to follow my nose, and to put the canoe into some brushy or boggy little stream that other hunters had—often but not always with good reason—overlooked. But in the end, I wound up doing most of my hunting on the Bay, and so becoming aware of how other hunters went about their business, and reluctantly recognizing that I had a lot to learn. I gradually became aware of how different the traditions and ethics of duck hunting were around the Bay from what they had been in South Carolina. It all began with the fact that hunting there was not a rich man's sport; it also owed a great deal to the old tradition of guiding, and to the feeling that came with it, that the Bay was a communal property, and that the hunters who used it were its de facto custodians, but were not and did not pretend to be its owners. They did not take the Bay for granted; they had an informed sense of the history of hunting there, which generally came to them from their fathers and grandfathers. The Bay to them was thus both a common—a place owned by no one—and a patrimony, an inheritance passed down to them. And when I talk to them, or go into their houses, I sense that it is something yet more basic and central, but less readily defined, than that.

LINWOOD RIDEOUT ASKED ME TO GO WITH HIM for a morning of hunting. This was more than a decade ago; Linwood had stopped guiding professionally, and did it strictly for pleasure. We put in at the Richmond landing a little before dawn and motored down to the foot of Swan Island, where he pushed the grass, while I sat in the front of the boat like a sport. It went well—three opportunities, three ducks: two mallards and a black, all in a couple of hours. This was a ratio of effort to result unprecedented in my duck-hunting experience.

At the end of the morning, we returned to Linwood's house by the Abby, where I'd left my truck, and while I was there he showed me his decoy collection. All were locally made, mostly from the years between the two World Wars, which were the years of his growing up, becoming first a hunter and then a guide, like so many of the local boys of his generation. That was an unprosperous time in Bowdoinham, even before the Great Depression arrived. The shipbuilding had played out; a calamitous fire had destroyed the town's waterfront of docks, warehouses, wharves, sawmills, and related enterprises. Agriculture was well into its long regional decline; and along every brook and stream you could have found evidences of old dams and mills, of a small-scale, homegrown economy, and with it, no doubt, of a certain kind of local morale that had gone south, or west, or just dried up and faded away.

But there were still plenty of ducks, and the Bay really came into its own as a duck-hunter's destination during Linwood's boyhood. "They used to have a saying," he said, "'The better the duck-hunting, the poorer the decoys.'" He laughed, "And you can see from what I've got here, the duck hunting was pretty fair in those days." It was true that his collection did not contain any of the beautiful specimens that have come to be considered as *objets d'art* and sold for five-and six-figure prices. Some looked like they had been made entirely with a hatchet, by a man who was in a hurry. Linwood's wife, Bid, took satisfaction in pointing these out. Her father, Earl Brown, had owned a popular sporting camp on Brown's Point, and he, like her husband, had guided and hunted on the Bay all of his life. She spoke of the decoys, and of duck-hunting generally, with a vigorous irreverence, in which heartfelt affection and heartfelt exasperation were inextricable. "Now look at that one. It's about my favorite—looks like a pelican, with maybe a little bit of elephant thrown in." Linwood said that was one of Frank Sieger's birds. "Whenever anybody teased Frank about his tollers, he said he wasn't after the smartest ducks. He was after the dumbest ones. 'Eliminate the dunces from the brood stock, and you'll improve the breed'—I'll bet I heard him say that a hundred times. But the quality of the decoy don't tell you much about the quality of the hunter." He took down a fat, oversized, blocky whistler. "Ronnie Burrell made this one, and there's not many better hunters than him."

As we talked, with him taking down decoys and passing them to me, then reshelving them as carefully as a librarian, putting each one back into its place, I realized I was getting a glimpse of a local history. "My father-in-law always said that if a guide was going to be ready for Opening Day, he had to start on the morning after the Fourth of July. And that by the end of August, there ought to be ten thousand blue-winged teal on the Bay. Now you're lucky to see a hundred or so. But the point is, you started aiming for Opening Day way ahead of time. We made a lot of decoys in this town—sit around on somebody's doorstep or in their barn after supper and whittle. You'd rough out the bodies with a hatchet, then shape them and make the heads with a crooked knife. We

didn't make 'em any fancier than they needed to be. They were equipment, like lobster pots or buoys. All of 'em were black duck decoys, more or less. Oh, you might slap a little white paint on the back in the second season, which was supposed to make 'em look like diving fowl—scaup or whistler. But black ducks were the prime bird. And every man had his own style—you could always tell whose decoy it was, just by looking at it."

The memory of all this pleased him. Heads, he said, were always getting broken, and were in great demand—every year, you'd make an extra supply of them, so that you could simply attach a new one to an old body, about like changing a tire.

I noticed that several of the decoys, while differing considerably, shared the same body style. They had obviously begun as a half-cylinder of wood. I asked him about them, and he took one down and handed it to me.

"See how light that is? White cedar. Floats high and it's easy to work. Back then, all the utility poles in town were white cedar, because it wouldn't rot. But they were weak, and it didn't take much to snap them. When the power company replaced a pole, they didn't haul it off, just left it lying beside the road. And if you saw one beside the road in the morning, you could bet it wouldn't be there when you came back by in the afternoon—somebody would have beat you to it. So you stopped right then, got out, sawed it up, and threw it in the trunk. You always carried a bucksaw with you in the

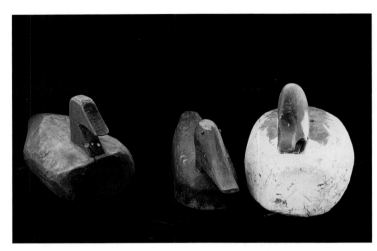

Folk art by (left to right) Wylie Munsey, Frank Siegers, Ronnie Burrell

Recycled utility pole. Linwood Rideout.

car, just in case. If it made you a little late for work, that didn't matter near as much as getting that pole did. I don't know if you could call leaving those poles by the road like that an act of good customer relations by the power company or not. But I can tell you, if they'd hauled 'em off, it would have been an act of *bad* customer relations. We regarded 'em as public property. Once, after a big snowstorm, I followed the Central Maine Power repair crew right up 201, from here to Richmond Corners. Got pretty much a lifetime's supply of decoy stock out of one blizzard—now that's what you call windfall profits."

He pointed out practical details about certain decoys— for example, that an exceptionally slender-bodied one had been built for use over toward the Woolwich side, or off of one of the points or islands in the main channel of the Kennebec, where the tide ran strongly, and a more conventionally shaped bird would have bobbed or swiveled in the current. But I was especially struck by several, which I mistakenly assumed were all the work of one carver. It turned out that Linwood himself had made some of them, and various of the Brown's Point Browns—Bid's people—had made the others. The bodies were what I could now recognize as recycled utility pole, and they looked too squat and short to me, as though the chief consideration had been to get as many decoys per pole as possible. But the heads compensated, and even overcompensated, for utilitarian, rudimentary designs of the bodies. They were highly stylized, slender and gracefully elongated, and there was evidence of a fussy, painstaking attention to detail that could have had no practical value—for example, a fine line inscribed around the outer edge of the beak, to distinguish the upper from the lower mandible.

I've thought about that particular decoy a good deal since—partly because of its pleasing combination of qualities, but also because it seemed to epitomize so many things. For one, a quietly competitive pride in craftsmanship—sitting around the barn or wherever it was, laughing and talking and having a fine time, you nevertheless wanted to turn out a distinctive product, something that expressed your sense of proportion and design, like anything else you built. You could look at Linwood's house, and at the tidy one-room camp he'd built right by the edge of the water to rent to hunters during the season, and see the same impulse at work—everything was neat, thrifty, well conceived, and satisfying to the eye.

The other thing, which I've subsequently met with in Buster, Adelbert, John Edgecomb, and the others, has to do with their whole sense of the birds they hunt and the place they hunt them. If you walk into their houses, you will see decoys—not the ones they use, which are out in the barn, or, in the season, already stashed in the gunning float, but a heterogeneous collection: some of them local, some of them picked up at an auction barn, some of them gifts or heirlooms, bequeathed to them by grateful hunters they had

guided for many years, or left to them by a favorite uncle, or inherited from their fathers. Buster's are displayed, with his usual neatness, on shelves built for the purpose along one wall of his living room. In other houses, they are placed here and there—one on a mantelpiece, three or four along the tops of the kitchen shelves. Some of them may be worth a good deal of money, but they are not given any special prominence. Duck hunting has created, as an accidental by-product, a local and a regional artistic tradition, and all of the hunters I've mentioned are both practitioners and connoisseurs of it. And if any artistic tradition matters to you, it is because it connects something inside of you to something that is outside of you.

For the actual hunting, Buster uses eight or ten oversized cork-bodied decoys, none of which appears to have its original head on it. Cork has the obvious advantage of buoyancy, but it breaks easily, and, when left in the bottom of the gunning float for the duration of the season, grows considerably waterlogged, so that by December some of Buster's decoys sit low and heavy in the water, more like loons than ducks. Their bodies have been patched with plastic wood or some similar filler, giving them the lumpy and battered appearance of old prizefighters. They do the job, in part because he knows exactly when and how to deploy them, and in part because he, like the others, is a skillful caller. But the other hunters rely largely on mass-produced synthetic decoys, which are light, tough, inexpensive, and lifelike. I thought John Edgecomb was at least a partial exception to this, as about half of his flock appeared to have cork bodies—exceptionally shapely ones. But he set me straight—he'd carved a solid wood body, sent it over to a metalworking shop in Lewiston and had a cast-aluminum mold made of it. Then he'd experimented with powdered Styrofoam until he found the right mix, and could produce a body that had the low gloss and high buoyancy of cork, and better weather resistance. It occurred to me that, if the tradition of duck hunting continued on the Bay and in his family, these decoys themselves might eventually become heirlooms, and move indoors. Like his gunning float, they represented a higher-tech version of a local craft. Their heads were traditional—white pine, very neatly whittled, sanded, and painted, identical to each other, and not identical to Buster's, or to the ones on the cork-bodied decoys that you can still buy, for a couple of arms and legs, at L. L. Bean's.

John, Jim Brawn, and Adelbert all load their own ammunition. This undoubtedly saves money, but it is also a way of extending the season, keeping in touch with the Bay even when it is frozen solid and Opening Day is a remote hypothesis. All are good shots—Adelbert, since he has retired from the well-drilling business, serves as a wing-shooting instructor over at Bean's, and wins statewide trap and skeet competitions from time to time. I suppose that a hunter who loads his own shells is like a trout fisherman who ties his own flies—there is a slightly experimental element in it. And the object of the experimentation is always to improve the ratio of ducks killed to ducks crippled, and therefore of ducks hit by shot to ducks recovered. I once remarked to John that the only part of duck hunting I didn't enjoy was the fact that, no matter how conservative you were about range, and how conscientiously you searched for birds you'd hit, you would always wind up crippling some birds and being unable to recover them—they'd escape by diving, or by getting into heavy cover. He agreed, and then thought for a minute. "Remorse is part of it, and you can't entirely eliminate it. You feel it even with the ducks you kill clean. And if a hunter doesn't feel it at all, he's got no business hunting."

I think that sense runs deep, and, as John says, it is inseparable from the pleasure and satisfaction of hunting on the Bay. When he was young, John got himself certified as a Maine Guide—it would be a good way of combining business with pleasure. "But then, when I had the license, I thought about it. It was like I had to get it before I could realize I didn't *want* to mix business and pleasure. I didn't want to risk spending a day out there with some guy I didn't like but had to be nice to, or some guy who didn't love duck hunting, whether the birds were flying or not. This thing's too important to me—I don't mind saying it's a thing I live for—and I don't want it mixed up with anything else."

Buster Prout builds his gunning floats and the oar that goes with each one; he keeps his well-used decoys in working order. But he goes beyond that. He builds precisely scaled models of his gunning floats, using precisely the same technique—beginning with garboard, transom, and prow, and attaching the strakes strip by strip. There can be no question of edge-nailing, because of the delicacy of the materials, and so he uses contact cement, which requires that each piece be set precisely in place the first time, without any tweaking or adjustment. He has made one-eighth-scale models for his nieces and nephews—he and Carol have no children of their own. When the model is finished, he equips it with a sculling oar, a set of goose decoys, and a Remington Model 870 shot-gun, all on the same scale as the float itself. Recently, he built a larger version—a one-quarter-scale boat. It cost him a lot of trouble, but came out a perfect, four-foot-long version of the boat I own. I asked him if he'd ever sold any of his mod-els. He said he couldn't—he'd have to ask too much for them. It had taken about as much time to build the four-foot model as to build a full-sized boat: it was worth too much to sell, and it would in some logically obscure but intuitively self-evident way be wrong to sell it for anything less than it was worth.

We value secular objects for the use we can make of them or the price we can get for them; we value sacred objects for what they are. The sacred ones we may insure if we are prosperous or sell if we are poor, but nothing replaces their meaning or their value. We know people who spend their lives seeking to make, acquire, or contemplate such objects, and we know people who spend their lives repudiat-ing them as evidence of superstition, snobbery, or silliness, as anachronistic as the gold standard.

Between these extremes there are objects that have acquired through long use and their many associations an intermediate status: Buster's old decoys perhaps have that status; and it was probably in honor of their desire to own and use such things that Linwood and his in-laws put those stylish, gratuitously detailed heads on their chunky-bodied decoys. But Buster's models move entirely away from the realm of utility. You would call them collector's items, but they are not for sale. They stand apart from the Bay's tradi-tions of boatbuilding and gunning, and from all of his own hours of waiting in the predawn darkness, or lying out flat and keeping calm, sculling the boat closer and closer to a flock of nervous, restive geese, or watching the shell ice crin-kle and flex as he motors through it, near the end of another season—they stand apart from his hours of doing that, and from those of three or four generations of hunters. And at the same time they epitomize and memorialize those things in a way that cannot and should not be separated from the painstaking, meticulous fidelity of their craftsmanship, or expressed in any other way, this essay included.

Red sky at morning

10/11

Hannah, our youngest daughter, had boarded the subway as usual on the morning of the eleventh, gotten out at her regular stop on Canal Street, and started walking west. At the first corner she had seen a small knot of people standing, looking down Broadway.

She was new to the city, new to the business of being a college graduate, a commuter, a person with a serious job. But she had learned enough to know that while small gatherings of spectators are not unusual in New York, they are not usual at rush hour. She got to the corner, looked, and saw what we have all now seen so many times.

Down the canyon of a city avenue, huge buildings, like mountains, appear to be both closer and smaller than they are. When she reached her office, she found it empty. She went to the window, raised the blinds, and saw that now each tower had a black hole in it, with more and more smoke billowing out of it. It still looked both closer and smaller than it was, and, in the beautiful clarity of a perfect autumn morning, egregiously unreal. The desks and computers and files, the coffee machine and the cups and saucers, the memos, telephones, and framed photographs at each work station, the Venetian blinds she had raised and the big plate-glass window itself—all those things were real and reassuring. What she saw outside seemed in another dimension, as though the window were a flat-screened television, one with brilliant optical resolution and no sound.

Her workplace got closed down for the rest of the week, and so on Friday she came home for a long weekend. I met her at the Portland bus station. Dark was just falling by the time we turned off I-95 and onto upper Main Street in Bowdoinham. For both of us, there was more emotion than usual about leaving the highway and entering this unselfconsciously pretty street. We drove by leafy, disheveled yards and houses that had a pleasant, unfussy, lived-in look, some occupied by people we knew and others so familiar to us that we felt almost acquainted with the strangers who inhabited them. Just before the street curved past the Church of the Nazarene and ran downhill to the village and the river, Hannah said, *"Oh. Look."*

Sitting cross-legged at the very edge of a yard were three teenaged girls. Each held a candle and huddled maternally over it, to shelter its wavering flame from the wind, the darkness, and the big world itself. They sat in a loose circle and their downturned faces, reflecting the soft light, looked the way candle-lit faces always do, luminous, pensive, and beautiful. We did not recognize the girls. Their anonymity linked them more powerfully than familiarity would have to the rev-elation of human solidarity, human fragility, awe, and selfless grieving that is the brief, sacred aftermath of tragedy.

And so we are at war. You would expect some translation into domestic policy of the willingness, and even the yearning, to share the burden of calamity that was so evident in this country after September 11. In the Second World War, those who did not go off to fight understood that sacrifices and inconveniences were in order. Food and fuel were rationed, victory gardens were promoted, an unprecedentedly steep rate of taxation was imposed upon the richest citizens. These were no doubt good, practical economic policies, but they were also good psychological and spiritual policies. They created a kind of civilian morale; they insisted that we forego our luxuries and reminded us that the shadow of war, like the shadow of death, was no respecter of persons; that we were all in it together. Of course the reality was much more compromised; of course the war did not create a Utopian interlude of genuine egalitarian neighborliness in the United States. But national policy did at least foster and sustain the idea of a common good and a common goal, and people who remember that time remember it with a certain pride.

We are told that the current struggle resembles World War II; that it is a struggle of good against evil, of civilization against barbarism, of a secular, tolerant, and humane pluralism against a theocratic, fanatical, xenophobic absolutism. But we are also told that those of us who are not directly involved in military operations can best serve the nation by resolutely spending money, on both essential and nonessential things. We are to act as though any reduction in our standard of living—in even our pleasure in the amenities enjoyed only by the most fortunate among us, in even our consumption of those resources (petroleum, for example) that are most essential to our national security and our military operations—were a symptom of weakness, a partial victory for our enemies.

Congress is presently considering the administration's economic response to the terrible events of September 11, a day that was said to have changed the world. But the economic response itself has been merely a continuation of what it had been before this great struggle began. It provides a bit more token relief for ordinary taxpayers, and massive tax advantages for corporations. It does not require the corporations to create new jobs, new facilities, or anything else that might alleviate a worsening economic situation at home or support our military efforts abroad. They are free to pass what amounts to a government subsidy directly on to their stockholders and their executives.

Over the course of my lifetime, which began in the early days of World War II, there has been a semantic shift no one seems to have noticed. Through my boyhood and into my young adulthood, we who inhabit this country and elect its officials were typically described as *citizens*. Now we hear that term much less often, and in its place we hear ourselves described as either the American taxpayer or the American consumer. *Taxpayer* suggests that we have no interest in government except the negative one of how much it costs us. *Consumer* suggests that we are addicted to acquisition, incapable of looking beyond the next trip to the mall, the next day's fix. In a time of crisis and sacrifice, our government seems intent only on deflecting the resentment of the taxpayer and perpetuating the consumer's habit.

WAR OR NO WAR, the duck season opened on the first of October. The moon was full on the second, and all the days and all the nights of the first week of the season were fair and unseasonably mild. I went out under the big moon, motored down to wherever I intended to hunt that morning, set my decoys, and waited on dawn. I did this almost every day of the first week of the season. The moon went from being full to being gibbous—to being half-full, or, strictly speaking, half-empty, since it was waning. Each night it was higher in the sky, farther above the western horizon, than it had been the night before. Motoring by moonlight on a still October night often means motoring in a silver mist, one that is sometimes thick enough to reduce you to groping around at half-throttle, hoping to find the loom of a familiar shoreline and so to get your bearings. But sometimes it means that a chilly little breeze stirs, dissipates the mist, and there is the moon above the black silhouette of the shore, its light a broad and glittering path across the water to you. The bow wake of the boat, reflecting and scattering this light across the water, is mesmerizing, and you can watch it until you feel that you are not moving at all, but are like a man seated beside a fountain, watching its spume surging and subsiding, surging and subsiding.

The old-timers are saying that the combination of warm weather, the full moon, and an exceptionally heavy rice crop was good for the ducks and bad for the hunters. The birds feed at night, clear out of the marshes an hour or two before sunrise, and sit out in open water, where they are safe as houses, until sunset. In any event, I did not have much shooting, which meant a lot of time to sit and take in the scene—to watch, for example, a pair of young eagles chasing each other low across the grass at the foot of Swan Island just as the sky was growing pale in the east. They came over me at less than treetop height, big and dark and portentous. I had a lot of time to think, if you can call it that, about how a huge and horrific event, even while it seems in one sense unreal, nevertheless affects the reality of the scene around you. I thought of what Hannah had said about the objects in her office that morning—how their ordinary reality had been a consolation, so much so that, when the order came for the building to be evacuated, she felt a powerful reluctance to leave them behind her.

Of the American anthems that have been played over and over this fall, the one that sounded right to me was "America the Beautiful," with its celebration of our astonishing geography, and of the redemptive power we have so often ascribed to it. Sitting in the boat through all the moment-by-moment alterations of morning light and driftings of mist, I thought of the New England luminists, painting in the mid-nineteenth century, in the context of a country that was developing a new kind of imperial arrogance and was pretty clearly headed toward either civil war or dissolution. The light that suffuses their work still shines on our October mornings—serene, delicate, and, although ephemeral, suggestive of that final peace which the Koran, the Talmud, and the Christian Bible all promise to their believers. To my eye, at least, the luminists did not conceive of that light as something that lay ahead of them, "at the end of the tunnel," but as something that lay behind them, an afterglow. It is very far indeed behind us now, and the light, however beautiful, is simply the light of another ordinary day. And suddenly we would gladly settle for that—another ordinary day.

The small, familiar objects in Hannah's office were more or less the same objects that, in the World Trade Center, were hurled outward by explosion or inhaled upward by thermal convection, and that would continue for days to drift down on the city like snow or ash, fragments of transactions, records, lives, and memories. The new war threatens all things, and so we see them in a new light.

Love of country embraces many things, and often the things are not loved until they are lost. War requires sacrifices; democracy requires that those sacrifices be shared. Those of us concerned with conservation need to be more concerned than ever. It seems clear that we shall not be asked to sacrifice our SUVs but our Arctic Wildlife Refuge; to jeopardize not global capitalism but the global environment. The national interest, the war effort, the spirit of bipartisan cooperation, our brave men and women who will be put in harm's way, and the terrible events of September will be invoked, all to discourage any questioning of what is being sacrificed, and for whom. And we will emphatically not be asked whether, given the choice, we would prefer to drill in Alaska or tighten our belts at home, to accelerate the depletion of our natural resources or to utilize them in more thrifty and considered ways.

IT IS IMPOSSIBLE FOR ME TO SPEND TIME on the Bay and not feel lucky to be an American. And even now, a month later, it is impossible for me to go down to New York and walk around lower Manhattan without feeling the same thing. That cantankerous, hyperkinetic welter of egos, cultures, neighborhoods, races, languages, and antipathies has somehow improvised an impressive human solidarity of compassion and fortitude, and lit candles as far away as Bowdoin-

ham. We are taxpayers and we are consumers, an odd combination of cynical suspicion and childish gullibility. But we have from time to time been called upon to show that we are more than that, and we have done so and can do so again.

As you motor back up the Androscoggin after a morning of hunting, you pass Cow Island, go under the new highway bridge connecting Route 1 to I-95, and then under the old iron railway bridge, with its dark, rusting girders and its granite piers. If, in these very strange times, you are looking for a sign to guide you, you will find it here. Toward the Brunswick end of the bridge, on its downstream side, there is some lettering in white paint. It is too neatly and carefully applied to be graffiti. It is chipped and faded and has been there for a long time. It seems to tell us as much as any of our officials can, and perhaps we should apply it to them, as well as to the amorphous shadows of death and danger that hang over us.

BE ADVISED, it says. Just that—nothing more.

Note:
This essay was written for the Friends of Merrymeeting Bay newsletter in the fall of 2001. I haven't altered or updated it: a part of whatever value it has comes from its being an immediate reaction to 9/11, written without benefit of hindsight.

Benefit of hindsight normally tends to decrease one's

sense of alarm and indignation, but in this case, it has the opposite effect. My essay underestimated the cynical opportunism of an incumbent administration, and the cowed acquiescence of its opponents, in pursuing, under the aegis of the war on terrorism, a preconceived agenda: such as the war against the environment; the war against privacy; the war against civil liberties and civility itself; the war, waged in the name of conservatism, against the conserving of anything. Except, of course, the wealth and influence of the wealthiest and most influential citizens.

Confluence

*E*ARL BROWN, LINWOOD'S *FATHER-IN-LAW, he had the sporting camps on Brown's Point, opposite to Darton's. Him and Darton didn't get on— not even a little bit. When I was a boy, be fooling around there by the Abby bridge, some fellow with Massachusetts plates would come along, see me, stop and ask me if this was the way to Darton's camps. Or to Brown's. It didn't matter—whichever one they were looking for, I sent 'em to the other. Just to stir the pot, you know. Old Man Earl finally figured out why he kept getting all these damn fellows looking for Darton's, and he gave me a pretty good cussing. He had a fair degree of talent in that line. But when I grew up a little more, he let me guide for him.*

But anyway, what we were talking about, to the best of my recollec- tion, was how the Bay's filled in. Now it was Earl's father, or maybe it would have been his grandfather, that come home from the Civil War, and first thing he did when he got home was set to work and build him his shad weir, right where he'd always had it. Just inside the tip end of Brown's Point, where there was a big back eddy. When he was doing it, he noticed she was shallower by a good deal than she'd been back before he went off. I think his name was Loyal Brown or Royal Brown, one or the other or something like it. Anyway, Loyal or whatever it was never took one shad out of that weir all spring. So what he does, he builds himself a platform, about ten foot high and out over the water, and he spent a lot of time on it, watching. He could see right down in the water. Now the water's a lot cleaner today than it was thirty-five or forty years ago, but t'ain't near as clean as it was back then. He could see the fish—shad and alewives—how they behaved, where they'd mill around while they were laying out of the current on a going tide. Next year, that's where he built his weir, and I heard he did all right for quite a few years after that.

I wish I could remember his name. I bet he wasn't more than eighteen or twenty years old when he went off to fight in that war. While he was down there, he got some kind of journal off a dead soldier. It must have been a Reb—seems like he'd have mailed it to that boy's parents if he'd been on our side. Probably no way to do that for a Reb, so he kept it and I guess he read it, because when the time came, he named his first boy after that fellow. And it might be that that was the one named Loyal or Royal or whatever, because that ain't a usual name around here as far as I know.

I believe he built that platform out there just about where that last pylon is at the end of Brown's Point. Somebody—probably Old Man Earl—pointed out to me where it was. And it's shallower off there now than it was back in Earl's day. He used to have a kind of bunker built into the bank along there. All grassed over in front and on top, and a sort of flap they could drop down to shoot. Linwood told me how it worked. Half a dozen or so fellows would be inside, playing cards, cooking, talking, and telling tales. One of 'em keeping watch. They had a big trawl of goose tollers set way out, and a cable running from them in to shore, and a winch there inside the bunker. When some geese would light in, they'd let 'em settle good, then start cranking, so all the tollers would start coming in toward shore, and all the geese swimming right along with 'em.

Everbody inside kept real quiet then—only guy who could see what was happening was the man at the crank—I guess he had some kind of slit he could peek out of. The rest of 'em got their guns and lined up along the wall, and when the man said the word, they dropped the flap and ever'body shot. Linwood said you didn't want to miss, especially if you planned for Earl Brown to be your father-in-law one day. It wasn't what you'd call sport. People in this town ate a lot of birds—blacks, geese, diving fowl—all through the winter. Breast 'em out and can 'em. A wonder I didn't lose my taste for 'em, but I never did.

Now I doubt that rig would've worked if the water in there was shallow as it is now. That ain't the case in every part of the Bay, though. Used to be that stand of grass off Center Point we called The Handkerchief. Good place. No grass at all out there now—the channel shifted I guess, and it's too deep.

T HIS WAS RONNIE BURRELL. He, John Lichter, and Buster had come to our house to talk over the just-completed season, and to check some data John had collected about migratory waterfowl populations against Ronnie's and Buster's memories. It was a cold night, and the stove was testifying. We sat around the dinner table with a big satellite photograph of the Bay laid out on it. It showed the Bay at a low tide. You could see all the flats and guzzles plainly; the shallows were a sort of milky blur, which gave all the fanned-out lobes and fingers of sand in the Androscoggin mouth the ghostly look of a chest x-ray. You could see a steam of muddier water coming out of the Eastern River into the Kennebec and hugging the Woolwich shore all the way down to the Chops, so you knew the tide was still falling. It took a minute for Buster and Ronnie to orient themselves to this unfamiliar perspective of a place they knew so well—I suppose it was like seeing your own house represented diagrammatically, by a drawing of its floor plan. But once they did, they could talk about changes in the Bay they'd seen, and changes described to them by the men who'd been old-timers to their generation. Our conversation wandered all over the photograph, and all over the map.

John Lichter has a tough job. Because the Bay is highly complex, and because systems of its type are so unusual, even the most basic facts of its hydrology have yet to be understood. The usual assumptions and generalizations about lakes, or about rivers, or about watersheds, or about coastal bays can be quite helpful or they can be quite misleading. And the Bay is a moving target, its dimensions, biology, and chemistry altered seasonally by freshets, floods, and equinoctial tides, altered over decades by human activity, altered over a longer time span by climactic and geological change. Records are at best unsystematic and incomplete; reliable base lines do not exist. Further, much of the Bay's most significant life is migratory—waterfowl and anadromous fish—and the ebb and flow of their populations around the Bay may indicate or result from changes in it, or may have to do

with conditions off the coast of Greenland, or in the breeding grounds of Canada. Invasive species—freshwater bass, brown trout, carp, catfish, loosestrife, fragmites—are wild cards.

The natural and human past of the Bay yields itself slowly. Ronnie listened closely—a habit he has—as John Lichter talked about taking core samples from the sediments, which could give him one kind of window on a millennium or so of what went on there. "I guess that's where the history of the Bay is written," Ronnie said to John, "but sounds like you've still got a lot of translation work ahead of you." So far, the translation is tentative. John had been surprised by how early the evidence of erosional sediments began showing up—within a few decades of the first European settlements in the area, a result of the clearing of the land, and of some big fires. The process continued and accelerated through the first half of the twentieth century. John was inclined to think that the larger history of the Bay confirmed Ronnie's story: it has grown shallower and more turbid. Both developments were probably good for the grass—siltation of topsoil increased the size of the intertidal zone and also its fertility. For the past half-century or so, this erosion has diminished—farming is playing out, up and down the rivers and around the Bay itself, and much agricultural land is reforested. This may explain something that all the old-timers have commented on—that the rice crop, while it has always

Kennebec River, downstream from the Chops

varied from year to year, isn't, on average, as good now as it was four or five decades ago.

You propose a theory as a tentative answer, but your real purpose is to raise new questions. If the intertidal zone had been smaller, and the rice less dense, before the European arrival, why had the Bay been so attractive to waterfowl in the pre-Colonial period? John thought it likely that the Bay had been far richer then than now in underwater vegetation, like the wild celery that had turned up in duck stomachs this fall. The water was clearer—quite possibly as clear as it still is in the lakes up north; therefore more sunlight could reach the bottom and nourish growth there. If the current trend continued, reductions in erosion would lead to increased water clarity, which might mean some recovery for aquatic plants.

But if that was true, why were diving ducks—scaup, goldeneyes, ringnecks—so much more common forty or fifty years ago than now? They had presumably been drawn to the Bay chiefly because of what they found below the surface—the vegetation that they ate, or that provided cover and sustenance for isopods and other small critters they fancied.

Well, John suspected from what he had learned about their doings in other places that carp might enter the equation. The literature suggested that they had a dire effect on aquatic plants, uprooting them as they scavenged around on the bottom, or feeding on them directly. And carp, it seemed, had really gotten established in the Bay sometime around the middle of the twentieth century, so their depredations would have more than offset the effects of greater water clarity. And they probably also fed directly on the crustaceans and mollusks that had been a big part of the Bay's attractiveness to diving fowl. They are not a game fish or a fish of any commercial importance in this state, and so their life cycle, feeding habits, and so forth have not been studied in a local context. We need to understand more about them, for sure—they are rooting around down there at the bottom of the food chain, and it is reasonable to suppose that they could affect the whole predatory hierarchy on the Bay, right up to the gunner in his float.

The history was written in mud and water, but also in other places. We can tell something about industrial and atmospheric contamination from traces of toxins that show up in John's core samples. And we can tell something about it from the eggs of eagles. In 1974 the United States Fish and Wildlife Service found DDT levels in an egg from Merrymeeting Bay that exceeded anything encountered in an eagle's egg anywhere else in the country. That, of course, was before the Clean Rivers Act had taken effect. But it would be a mistake to assume that the subsequent news has all been good. In 1991–92 a study found high levels of a variety of toxins in eagles' eggs from nests around the Bay, and the levels of dioxin and related compounds in one egg from a nest in Bowdoinham were higher than anything *ever found in the tis-*

sue of any organism anywhere—more than 2,000 percent above the threshold for damage to the organism. We cannot know whether this indicates long bioaccumulation in the parent birds, or what the proximate and ultimate sources of the toxins are. We can only know that this, too, is a kind of chronicle—the kind that lets us know that, for all the environmental gains that we have made, we have not erased the legacy of abuse. Do the carp, disturbing the fine sediments in which toxins are likely to be especially concentrated, put them back into circulation? What is the effect of floods or periods of sustained high water, such as we had this fall?

John Lichter does not do optimism, and he does not do pessimism. He only wants to find out, as best he can, how things stand, and how they stood. That is a big, complicated task, and it will require not only his personal commitment and that of other scientists, but also the kind of sustained commitment that only institutions—state or federal agencies, colleges, universities, private laboratories, and so forth—can insure. This work is still in its very early days, but at least it has begun, and the people who do it do it in the faith that it will continue.

In the kitchen that night, we stood over the table and looked at the photograph. We talked a good deal about the Big Flats at the mouth of the Eastern. The rice there has been poor for quite some time, even in years when it was good elsewhere on the Bay. It is generally thin, and seems to fall down very early—by the beginning of October less than half of it is standing. The Big Flats happened to be the first place on the Bay that I'd hunted, and I hunted there pretty regularly thirty and thirty-five years ago. Ronnie and Buster were right—the rice had been much thicker then. It came to me as a bit of a surprise to remember that, because I had not hunted there every year, as they had, and had only slowly learned to notice and register such things. Recollection is not exactly random, but it often relies on some external stimulant—something that reminds memory and brings it back to life.

The history of the Bay is a matter of analyzable data contained in sediment and tissue; a matter of written records, some published, and none systematic or comprehensive, and it is a matter of memory. I liked sitting in the room, looking at the map, and listening to these efforts to correlate data and recollection; I especially liked the way that Ronnie's memory circled away from the subject and then circled back to it. I didn't have a scientist's obligation to try, insofar as was possible, to produce a coherent account. I thought to myself that the one thing I was sure to remember from this evening was the story about Loyal/Royal Brown and the Civil War, the dead boy, the dead boy's journal, and the remorse or magnanimity that led Brown to perpetuate his name. That memory was now also a place out near the end of Brown's Point where there had been a shad weir—Brown

Discovery

probably spent a lot of time, down there in Virginia, missing things like shad weirs, and dreaming about the life that had once been ordinary for him.

So. This terminates an incomplete, uncomprehensive, unsystematic book. I will conclude lamely by telling you that you really just need to go and see for yourself. To do that, you will need a boat—a canoe would be best, but a kayak will do fine, or a light skiff. And you will need a day in late September. Plan it out ahead, and consult the tides. If the tide is low, just beginning to rise, and the wind is still, you might want to consider starting in Bath and riding the tide up the Kennebec and through the Chops. Or you could start in Brunswick where the tide continues to fall for another hour or so after it has already begun to rise in the Bay proper. There is a maze of islands and back channels, pretty places, along that route. If the tide is high and beginning to fall, you could start at the town landing in Bowdoinham. The Cathance between the landing and the Bay is a nice enough stream, and there's something breathtaking and uplifting about the way it rounds a final tight corner at the end of Wildes Point and opens out into the Bay, with Brick Island straight ahead, the Muddy River coming in on the right, and Pleasant Point, handsomely wooded, jutting into the big marsh between the Muddy and the Androscoggin. There's a big marsh on the left as well, a double-lobed cove shaped like

a handwritten lowercase *m*. Or, on falling water, you could begin in Richmond. Even though it means bucking the current for a short distance, you should go upriver a little way, so that you can round the north end of Swan Island and come down its eastern side. The small channel between Swan and Little Swan, winding and deeply shadowed by big trees on both sides, is not to be missed.

If you are ambitious, and have time, bring camping gear and spend the night on Brick Island. It is a de facto public camping place, and a very pretty one—a small island, an open glade among surprisingly tall and upright pines.

If you are pressed for time, or unsure whether you want to invest this much of it in a place that has no cachet as a tourist destination, you have my permission to go to east Bowdoinham, turn off to the right just before you get to the little bridge over the Abby (to the left, and just after the bridge, if you are coming from the Richmond direction) and go out Center Point for about a mile, then turn left at mailbox number 148. This will take you down to the unofficial landing on the Abby where John Lichter, his students, and I began and ended our duck-census operations this past fall and where many falls ago Ronnie stood and saw the eagle and the swan. You are within half an hour's easy paddle of the place I would recommend, first and foremost, to anybody desiring a preliminary acquaintance with the Bay, something that will indicate to them whether they should consider a long-term relationship. As you paddle out, Bluff Head Cove—where the dastardly Darton tried to monopolize the hunting—will be on your right; on your left will be Brown's Point, the center of opposition to Darton's scheme.

If the tide is low—on the whole, that might be best— follow the southward curve of the Abby channel out to the Sands, pull your boat up onto the beach, and get out. Be sure to anchor the boat, or at least jam a paddle into the sand and tie up to it, before you set off to explore, or to take a swim—the water in September is still quite comfortable, unless there's been a lot of rain. Keep an eye on the tide—it comes fairly quickly here, once it starts. But also keep an eye on the water further out—there's always a chance of a short-nosed sturgeon jumping for you, or of a cloud of gulls and terns and a school of stripers. Study the sky too, high and low, for evidence of harriers, an eagle or two, a peregrine, or an osprey. It is possible you will see nothing at all, but the odds don't favor it. If you've brought a sandwich, or just an apple or a bottle of water, now is the time for it.

As the tide begins moving in strongly, cutting through the guzzle between the beach and the marsh behind it, get back into your boat and let the tide carry you upriver, along the outer fringe of the big marsh that stretches from the Sands almost to Brown's Point. There are several guzzles along here, some going all the way through to the Abby, some playing out. I think you ought to bypass the first two

or three of these, and wait until you are approaching Brown's Point to turn up into the grass. If there's just water enough to paddle, that's perfect. If not, you can wade—the center of the channel, scoured by the current, is firm and sandy underfoot.

As you advance, you will begin flushing ducks. There are not as many as there once were, but there are enough for our purposes. The teal skim low over the grass; the blacks and mallards climb higher, sort out their ranks, and arrange themselves in long strings or loose chevrons. The further you go, the more you flush. Many will seem now not to be flushing in response to you, but to the birds already in flight above them, as though that many wings in the air was enough to trigger their seasonal restlessness. They mill around in the sky, pitch back down in a far corner of the marsh, or rise from there, jumpy and panic-prone as stockbrokers. You can almost pick up the rumors of hunting season and of winter that spread among them, but for the moment, they are here in front of you, beautiful in the sunlight.

There is a lot to be said about them; I've said some of it. They imply much. They have economic importance; they are the subject of state and federal legislation and of state and federal politics. Their numbers should be of concern not only to hunters and conservationists but to us all. They are an index of the environmental history and environmental health of this bay, this nation, and this hemisphere. But when you look at them, don't think too much about that. Think instead about what this scene would be like without them— the marsh, the sky, the water, the wooded shores—still something beautiful, but with the empty, silent beauty of a photograph. What would be missing would be something inside yourself—a kind of elation, a sensation, within your solitude, of a happy conviviality, a meeting that takes place only here, at this confluence of rivers and flyways and seasons, of fresh water and salt, of natural history and human history, and the one life you'll ever have.

Cathance River: High summer, high tide

Late summer: Ripening rice, dimpling rain

Greenwing teal, September rice

October

November: Fallen and matted rice

Winter: Deer crossing to Swan Island

Spring: Mouth of the Abby

Quabacook: Black duck and floe ice